Sealink
and before

Ferry
Publications

John Hendy

Justin Merrigan

Bruce Peter

Introduction

This book celebrates in words and pictures, the 36 years of British Railways' shipping services, latterly trading as Sealink. On New Year's Day 1948, the 'Big Four' railway companies came together to form a single Nationalised concern but whereas the railway aspect of this event has been well documented, their shipping services, which BR also inherited, have received rather less attention.

Initially the new railway's maritime activities were operated on a regional basis but in 1969 they were merged and came under the wing of the British Railways Shipping & International Services Division (S&ISD) after which time the larger ships tended to be designed to serve on a multiplicity of routes rather than being purpose-built for a specific crossing. These were often difficult years for the operator as financial constraints and railway oriented managers frequently failed to provide the tonnage necessary to compete with opposition companies or, more importantly, to judge the overall trends in a rapidly changing market. The roll on - roll off revolution from the mid-1960s found much of the fleet both out of date and out of touch. French, Belgian

and Dutch partners later joined the Sealink consortium and also suffered from similar problems.

The S&ISD adopted the trading name 'Sealink' and 10 years later became Sealink UK Ltd. Privatised in 1984 and then subject to a hostile takeover in 1990, the name 'Sealink' was finally dropped in 1996 but by then the world had moved on and the versatile and diverse British Rail fleet and all that it represented had largely passed into history.

In 2014 'Ferry Publications' produced 'Sealink and Beyond' which follows the fortunes of the company and its ships after the 1984 privatisation. This present book introduces its readers to the BR fleet in 1948 and traces its course throughout the years of Government control right through until the time of its denationalisation.

A final word of thanks to Miles Cowsill of Ferry Publications for designing the book.

John Hendy, Justin Merrigan, Bruce Peter
October 2015

Acknowledgements

Many people have greatly assisted the authors by delving into their collections to share photographs with a wider audience. In particular we would like to thank Jim Ashby who continues to be an enthusiastic ambassador for Sealink long after retirement from the ferry business. Don Smith, of Phototransport, is also thanked as is Ken Larwood who enthusiastically answered the call of help. Appreciation also to Ronnie Roberts, Nigel Thornton, August Goethals, Michael Woodland, Mark Leiper and David Heath. A special word of thanks is due to the Manchester Locomotive Society for access to the collection of the late J. Wallace Sutherland and to FotoFlite at Ashford for access to their wonderful collection.

Contents

Produced and designed by Ferry Publications trading as Lily Publications Ltd
PO Box 33, Ramsey, Isle of Man, British Isles, IM99 4LP
Tel: +44 (0) 1624 898446   Fax: +44 (0) 1624 898449
www.ferrypubs.co.uk   E-Mail: info@lilypublications.co.uk

Printed and bound by Printer Trento, Italy
© Ferry Publications 2015

The *Earl Leofric* on passage to Calais from Dover. *(FotoFlite)*

CHAPTER ONE

Development

Britain emerged from the Second World War victorious, but physically badly damaged and heavily indebted. On the home front, the nation's transport infrastructure had borne the brunt of the conflict and was worn out. At the 1945 General Election, the two main political parties espoused opposing solutions to this problem. The Conservatives, supported by the 'big four' railway companies – the London & North Eastern Railway, the London Midland & Scottish Railway, the Great Western Railway and the Southern Railway – suggested nationalising railway infrastructure, then charging 'line rental' to train operating companies (a solution imposed half a century later). Labour, on the other hand, supported nationalising the railways in their entirety. Across a wide range of issues it caught the national mood, winning a landslide victory – but, in the King's Speech, no mention was made of transport; then – as now – health and education were seen as the greatest vote-winners and so another two years passed before a major transport policy initiative was developed. In the interim, the 'big four' struggled on as best they could, the unreliability of rail and sea services reflecting the wider austerity conditions of the era.

For the war's five-year duration, most of the railway steamer fleet had seen military usage, vessels and their crews serving with distinction as mine-sweepers, troop transports and hospital ships; many of the railway companies' estuarial steamers had taken part in the evacuation of Dunkirk, when several became war casualties. In the war years, only skeletal domestic services were maintained by the few vessels not called up for naval auxiliary duty. Those that were returned to the railways at the war's conclusion were in a very dilapidated condition and, while some were extensively renovated and returned as quickly as possible to civilian service, others were too badly degraded and were instead written off to be consigned for scrapping.

After the war, the railway companies immediately placed orders for new tonnage – but the new vessels commissioned were little different from their pre-war predecessors. For example, the replacement LMS Stranraer-Larne car ferry *Princess Victoria* was nearly identical to her 1930s namesake, while a new LNER Clyde paddle steamer, the *Waverley*, was conceptually little different from tonnage built from the 1890s onwards. For the Harwich-Hook of Holland night service, the LNER commissioned the *Arnhem*, a well-appointed turbine steamer, but one very much in the 1930s railway idiom.

Under the provision of the Transport Act 1947, Britain's railway systems were brought under Government control on 1st January 1948 and the shipping arms of the 'big four' were absorbed into the British Transport Commission (BTC) under the control of the Railway Executive. Shipping services were administered by each of the six new railway regions of British Railways; these were the Southern Region, Western Region, London Midland Region, Eastern Region, North Eastern Region and the Scottish Region. The new national railway's strong regional structure maintained the existing management infrastructures of the 'big four', resisting attempts by the BTC to seize control to the centre.

The new British Railways was positively welcomed by most of the British populous and there was a hope that, with investment, brighter days would lie ahead. The early re-introduction of luxury Pullman trains after the war injected some much needed glamour into the dilapidated system and, equally, the rejuvenated steamer fleet – offering continental travel to a

PORT TO PORT

The ships owned and operated by British Railways offer a reliable and regular cross Channel service every day throughout the year

A wonderfully evocative advert from 1958, promoting the shipping services of British Railways. The image portrays professionalism, playing on the words port to port describing not only the nature of the business but also the action taken by two ships approaching head on to pass each other safely. *(Jim Ashby collection)*

fortunate few – appeared to represent the aspirational end of railway operations. A 1948 British Transport film, entitled 'Golden Arrow' captures the mood of the era. The film begins with the stirring sight of an immaculately turned out 'Merchant Navy' class 'Pacific' locomotive, hauling renovated Pullman cars of pre-war vintage out of London Victoria, bound for Dover. Meanwhile, at the town's Western Docks, the Channel steamer *Invicta* is being prepared for the arriving passengers. She is introduced as:

"…A ship with most honourable war service to her credit. From the earliest hours, the *Invicta*'s crew have been busily preparing for our coming. Decks have been scrubbed immaculate with water from the cold salt sea and, with commendable energy, brasses have been polished in true nautical fashion so that they reflect the perfection of the service. So that the pangs of hunger need never assail the Golden Arrow's passengers, stores and victuals that will later grace *Invicta*'s tables have been loaded in readiness for the crossing… White-starched cooks – the 'galley slaves' as they call themselves – have been preparing a meal whose appeal none can deny… And there she lies – fresh and glowing, awaiting the fortunate travellers' arrival. All the experience of the merchant navy gives the certainty of our safe arrival on the other side of the Channel…"

Viewers are invited to make a connection between the pride and professionalism with which the railway packet steamer is operated and the equal expertise underpinning Cunard's grandest trans-Atlantic liners.

The *Invicta*'s sunny crossing of the Dover Strait appears idyllic – more like a short cruise; passengers smoke, dine, sip cocktails and sunbathe while children run around the decks – a carefree shipboard world, at once close, yet far away from the dangers of the recent conflict. As the vessel approaches Calais, the after-effects of the war become poignantly evident; apart from the silhouette of the hôtel de ville, the town has been razed by bombardment into a flatscape. At the port, customs inspections take place in a temporary shed before passengers join the French 'Flèche d'Or' for Paris.

The *Invicta*'s 'Golden Arrow' service represented the very best that the BTC's post-war steamer fleet could offer. Elsewhere, the vast majority of 'ordinary' passengers, not travelling in Pullman luxury, had a very different view of shipping operations. On the Clyde, so many steamers had been lost, or found upon demobilisation to be beyond redemption that

only a very basic service was offered – and the shipboard catering often left much to be desired. The Clyde steamer historian Iain C. MacArthur records the standard of catering in the difficult post-war years of austerity:

"Catering suffered severely as a result of the war; but main meals of some sort could be had in all the ships even during the worst period of wartime and post-war food rationing... By the beginning of 1951, the catering was still short of the standards both of pre-war years; but it was well beyond the stage at which the main course of lunch served on board *Duchess of Fife* in April 1947 consisted of wartime M&V (tinned meat, vegetables and gravy). As late as June 1951 bacon and egg for high tea was sufficiently rare to be remembered..."

The resolve of the British Transport Commission's management to wrest more control of shipping from the regions to the centre was stiffened by the unexpected sinking on 31st

such as ships for the railway fleet. It was for this reason that in 1954 Colonel Frank Bustard's Atlantic Steam Navigation Company was nationalised. Its founder, Frank Bustard, was an avowed believer in private enterprise but, as his bankers refused to grant loans to pay for new tonnage, being absorbed by the BTC was the 'least worst' option. As the BTC also owned British Road Services, a major freight forwarding company with a large fleet of trucks, the acquisition of Bustard's freight ferry fleet enabled 'door-to-door' haulage services to be provided under single overall administration.

In 1955, post-war rationing finally was ended and the Government announced a far-reaching Modernisation Plan for Britain's railways; steam haulage was to be replaced, region by region, with new diesel and electric trains. The Modernisation Plan also offered the promise of new vessels for the BTC's fleet. Sensing that large sums of money were about to be offered to

Looking aft from the bridge wing on Stranraer's **Antrim Princess**. Flying from her cross trees, the Caledonian Steam Packet Co. house flag. *(Bruce Peter collection)*

The foredeck of the car ferry **Avalon**. *(Kenny Whyte)*

January 1953 of the recently introduced Stranraer-Larne ferry *Princess Victoria*. In stormy conditions, the vessel's car deck flooded and, as a result, she suffered a rapid capsize with the loss of 128 lives. As a result, the BTC formed the view that the shipping services should be separated from railway management. This was, however, strongly resisted by the Railway Executive who favoured a single international transport system with shipping services closely integrated with connecting rail services. This, along with other major disagreements, led to the abolition of the Railway Executive from 1st October 1953 through the Transport Act 1953.

The Conservative Government elected in 1951 promised to encourage entrepreneurship to cut Britain's accumulated burden of debt – but, in practice, so far as transport and the other nationalised industries were concerned, it perpetuated a post-war consensus that public ownership was best. There was a very practical reason for this; finance was in short supply and only the Government could afford to invest in expensive assets,

the BTC, the main drivers' union, ASLEF, called a lengthy and acrimonious rail strike. This took place at a time when Britain's expanding middle class was beginning to enjoy new signs of prosperity – buying a car being an obvious status symbol and an enabler of personal freedom with which rail travel could not easily compete (back then, there was plenty of unused road space). Growing car ownership would have a profound influence on governmental policy towards the railways – and, so far as shipping operations were concerned, would necessitate the building of numerous new car ferries.

A distinguishing feature of car ferries – as opposed to passenger-only steamers whose clientele arrived by train – was their one-class of accommodation, it being assumed that, as all motorists were likely to be solidly middle class, none would indulge in indecorous behaviour and so there would be no need to separate 'First' from 'Third Class'.

With more car ferries shortly to be ordered, the BTC formed a new Naval Architecture Department in December 1956,

On relief duty at Rosslare is the car ferry **Holyhead Ferry I**. *(David Heath)*

capable of imposing uniformly high engineering and operational standards across the entire railway fleet. Initially, this was headed by Leslie Harrington, assisted by Don Ripley who was appointed Chief Draughtsman. The Principal Naval Architect was Philip Salisbury. In an effort to create further efficiencies the Shipping and International Services Department was established at the BTC in January 1957, but the regions were still responsible for the operation of shipping. As part of the 1955 Modernisation Plan, a Design Panel was established to hire consultants to advise British Railways about the design of documentation, rolling stock, stations and new ships. While many railway traditionalists sought to resist – or ignore altogether – industrial design advice, the naval architects were at least willing to collaborate. A new Dover Strait car ferry, the *Maid of Kent*, delivered in 1959, was hailed as being an outstanding example of an integrated approach to engineering, interior design and graphics.

As a consequence of the 1955 rail strike and the BTC's

Serving the passenger

Passenger comfort and travelling amenities are the top priorities in the new trains of the sixties. Some, like the Glasgow Blue Trains of the Clydeside electric service, have already proved how well good design pays in terms of greatly-increased revenue within a relatively short time. Another successful new service, the Midland Pullman, has managed to win back passengers from air travel

Simple, 'unfussy' outlines, brighter colours, more space and light per passenger, a smoother ride in a vehicle that not only looks clean but is easy to keep clean - these are the main elements in modern British train design. It makes full use of the advantages of modern materials and production techniques.

Ships

The corporate identity is being extended to the British Rail fleet of over 100 ships. Here, too, the symbol lends an air of continuing purpose in the combination of the colours of pale grey, blue and flame red. The sea voyage is seen to be what it is - an extension of the rail journey

A page from British Rail's corporate identity manual showing the new livery adopted in 1964/65 as applied to Holyhead's cargo and cattle ship *Slieve Donard*. *(Justin Merrigan collection)*

ever-increasing deficit, the Government however lost faith in the railways. There were, after all, more votes to be gained by encouraging car owners through investment in new roads. Prime Minister Harold Macmillan appointed Ernest Marples (formerly of the Marples-Ridgway construction company, a firm that specialised in road building) as his Transport Secretary. Marples set about 'reforming' the BTC with enthusiasm. During the early 1960s, British Railways underwent a radical reorganisation. By the Transport Act 1962 the Transport Holding Company was established to take over the business of the BTC, which was dissolved. The British Railways Board was formed on 1st January 1963 with the BTC's Chairman, Dr Richard Beeching, appointed as Chairman. The report 'The Reshaping of British Railways' was published later that year and in it the BRB presented a plan for a new, more efficient, and smaller service to counteract what was seen as an uneconomic operation.

The Shipping and International Services Department survived the ending of the BTC and became part of the BRB's organisation with a general manager and support staff reporting to a board member. The regions' responsibilities were not altered by this reorganisation. The BRB took over the BTC's shareholdings in the Caledonian Steam Packet Company, Caledonian Steam Packet Company (Irish Services) Ltd, Fishguard and Rosslare Railways and Harbours Company and Société Anonyme de Navigation Angleterre-Lorraine-Alsace subsidiaries. The BRB also inherited shares in these companies owned by the Société Belgo-Anglaise des Ferry Boats (SABTC) passed to the new BRB. The BTC's shares in three further shipping subsidiaries – Associated Humber Lines Ltd, Atlantic Steam Navigation Company Ltd and David MacBrayne Ltd – passed to the Transport Holding Company.

The BRB Chairman Dr Beeching sought to make British Railways more efficient and was easily persuaded by the railway Design Panel that a rebranding would be a cost-effective way of achieving an appearance of modernisation – after all, paint and transfers were relatively cheap and the railway's existing 'heraldic' image looked antiquated in the jet age and the 'swinging sixties'. This rebranding happened against a background of extensive pruning of the rail network to save money – and so the snappy new brand identity of British Rail, first introduced in 1964/65, was perceived by satirists as an appropriately shortened name for a severely truncated network. As the railway shipping fleet was repainted on an annual basis,

it was the first aspect of the BRB's activities where the new corporate identity and 'double arrow' logo made a major impact (trains and stations were rebranded over a ten-year period). On the newest car ferries, the British Rail livery of monastral blue hull, pale grey (later, white) superstructure and flame red funnel casing with 'double arrow' made a positive impact – but the same livery looked faintly absurd when applied to vintage Humber and Isle of Wight paddle steamers with slim, tall 'steamer' funnels. In Scotland, the Caledonian Steam Packet Company's management strongly resisted the new identity and so the Clyde steamer fleet retained the existing buff yellow funnel livery, albeit with the addition of lions rampant as a logo (while hulls were repainted in monastral blue).

British Railways and its continental partners on the Dover Strait already faced competition from Townsend, whose ferry operation had been established specifically to court motorists. As the 1960s progressed, other ferry entrepreneurs established

Resting at Fishguard, the **St David**. In the days before bow thrusters, the stern lines will assist the ship off the berth as she turns 90 degrees to steer out of the harbour. *(David Heath)*

themselves in competition with railway-owned vessels, for example Thoresen Car Ferries on the Channel and Western Ferries in Scotland.

The regions finally lost the control of shipping on 1st January 1968 when the Shipping and International Services Division was formed. The division was responsible for all British Rail shipping services, railway-owned ports and the development of traffic and liaison with continental and Irish railway administrations. Management for the Stranraer to Larne service was transferred

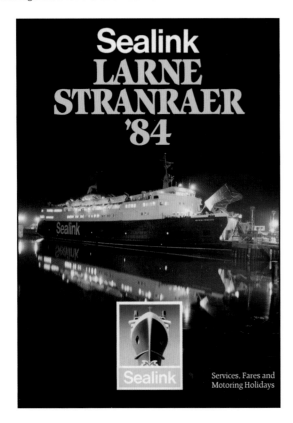

from the Caledonian Steam Packet Company (Irish Services) Ltd to British Transport Ship Management (Scotland) Ltd. Clyde and Hebridean ferry and excursion steamer services meanwhile passed from the railways to the Scottish Transport Group, the parent company of the Scottish Bus Group, further reflecting the ongoing shift in emphasis from rail to road as Britain's prime means of mobility; in 1973, the Caledonian Steam Packet Company and David MacBrayne fleets were merged and renamed as Caledonian MacBrayne. At the same time as these changes, the S&ISD, along with the shipping services of the continental railways, began marketing its services under the brand name 'Sealink'.

British Rail may have been hasty in disposing of steam railway traction, but it was slow to make a similar move in shipping. Indeed, during the mid-sixties, turbine steamers continued to be introduced, such as the 1965 Irish Sea vessel *Holyhead Ferry I* – the name of which was derided for its banality – and the near-sister *Dover* for the Channel route to Boulogne. The first large BR motor ships, the *Antrim Princess* for the Stranraer-Larne route and the Harwich-Hook of Holland vessel *St George* – appeared only in 1968. The prospect of diesel propulsion rather than steam did not go down well with one Captain who, only half-jokingly, commented to the naval architects that "I believe you are building a Deeeeesel ferry... I have no desire to be propelled across the Channel by a series of explosions." As well as investing in up-to-date roll-on, roll-off tonnage, British Rail also expanded its container services, building a new facility at Harwich (inaugurated in 1968), served by two purpose-built container ships, the *Seafreightliner I* and the *Seafreightliner II*. One of the principal containerised cargoes was Ford car parts, which were shipped between the Dagenham factory in East London and Ford's continental car plants.

In the latter 1960s, BR decided to name new ships after characters from Medieval history – such as *Vortigern* (1969), *Hengist*, *Horsa* and *Senlac* (1972-73). Instead of commemorating such Dark Age warriors, subsequent new buildings took the names of saints – for example the Harwich-Hook of Holland ferry *St Edmund* (1974) and the sturdy Irish Sea vessel *St Columba* (1977) for the Holyhead-Dun Laoghaire route.

British Rail ownership of shipping services continued through the 1970s. The 1973 Oil Crisis, which followed Arab OPEC members' decision to quadruple the price per barrel of Gulf Crude, led to an urgent need to replace the remaining steam turbine vessels with diesel tonnage – but, as there was insufficient funding forthcoming, an alternative approach was to charter tonnage instead. Since the mid-1960s, Stena Line had provided a variety of vessels for BR routes, beginning with the *Stena Nordica* between Stranraer and Larne. During the 1970s, Stena provided numerous passenger and freight vessels to supplement BR's fleet, few members of which had enough space for trucks or trailers.

The Sealink fleet of the mid-1970s was mainly of recent vintage, few of the larger units being more than 20 years old – but, notwithstanding its modernity, what the travelling public experienced varied greatly in terms of quality. Service standards often depended on the motivation of particular crews, some vessels being well turned out while others were sadly neglected. In 'Designing Ships for Sealink', the naval architects Don Ripley and Tony Rogan recalled that some of the crew on the Channel Islands ferry *Earl Granville* were frustratingly lethargic with regard to maintenance:

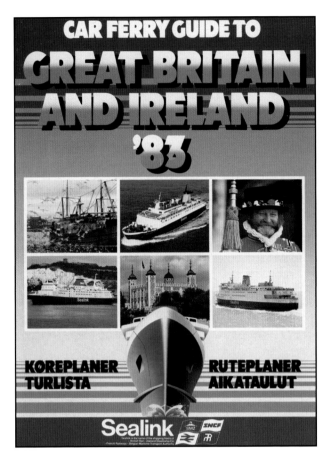

An artist's impression of the **Manx Viking** in the new Sealink livery adopted in 1984. In reality, the ship never wore these bold colours, instead being sold despite being ear marked for service at Weymouth as the 'Earl Henry'. *(Jim Ashby collection)*

"Looking around the public spaces… while preparing the specification for modifications, Don was asked by some stewards who were sitting in the restaurant having a cup of tea before passengers came on board, whether he could include in the work the securing of wobbly table tops… Don got under one of the tables, had a look at the securing of the top to the base and suggested that if they drank less tea and used a screwdriver for five minutes, the table tops would not wobble. They had the good grace to admit that he was right and that if the table was in any of their homes they would have done it automatically. There have been many such instances but we must also point out that there have been at least an equal number where crew members have made repairs and improvements with no other thought than making it a little bit more their ship."

A search in the Times Digital Archive for Sealink-related reportage and correspondence produces three main categories – industrial disputes, double-figure fare rises and complaints about dirt and poor service. The 1970s was a period notorious for its poor labour relations and Sealink's officers, crews or dock workers not infrequently went on strike to achieve enhanced pay settlements. The 1973 Oil Crisis quadrupled the cost of fuel – and acted as a catalyst for high inflation in the economy as a whole – so, to offset greatly increased operating costs, Sealink increased fares by between 12 and 15 per cent. Some peak fares nearly doubled, The Times' travel correspondent John Carter observing that in the summer of 1976, a family of four in a car would have paid £74 for a Dover-Calais return crossing, whereas only a year later, the cost was £114. Shortly thereafter, Carter's colleague, Patricia Tisdall reported the results of an independent survey of ferry companies, which found Sealink's British vessels to be characterised by:

"Poor standards of cleanliness… Holidaymakers in the Midlands complained to researchers that Sealink ferries were filthy [and] in the case of breakdown, passengers had to wait on the quay without meals until repairs were carried out for 11 hours in one instance."

By contrast, vessels operated by Brittany Ferries, Townsend Thoresen, Hoverlloyd, Tor Line, SNCF and RMT met with almost universal approval. In a 1975 article, The Times reported on the over-booking of a Sealink Irish Sea crossing from Holyhead. One intending passenger, the Deputy Mayor of Camden, complained:

"The whole thing was monstrous and a national disgrace. The Toilets [at Holyhead] constitute a health hazard, there are no catering arrangements, there is no hot water… The nearest telephone is half-a-mile away and I had to walk nearly a mile to get a cup of coffee for an old-age pensioner. The British people have tolerated these dreadful conditions for years; I wonder what impression foreign visitors take away with them."

A British Rail spokesman responded to this tirade with the observation that the Deputy Mayor and other passengers had turned up at the wrong port as, according to Sealink's records, they were supposed to be sailing from Fishguard.

A disappointed Dover Strait passenger, meanwhile, felt moved to write to The Times' letters page to record the following:

"Sir – On a recent trip across the Channel on the British Rail Sealink vessel, the *Maid of Orleans*, I had occasion to be sitting up on the deck eating lunch, due to the fact that it was overcrowded downstairs and I could find nowhere to sit. As I sat there, I watched with fascination as two of the crew emerged from below carrying between them a dustbin full of rubbish from the buffet, walked past four giant rubbish containers standing on the deck, and calmly tipped the contents over the side of the boat. What price 'pollution-free' travel now?"

It was not all bad news, however. In 1977, Holyhead got a much needed boost thanks to the introduction of the new and well-appointed *St Columba*, "twice the size of its predecessors and lavishly endowed with those amenities – bars, lounges, shops, restaurants, disco, television, comfortable seating and attractive furnishing – which have become the norm on other routes." The Times' correspondent, Michael Bally went on to explain that:

"The Irish Sea crossing is not like others around the British coast, an indication of which is not only that it is only at this late stage that it is getting a comparable ship, but that against the trend elsewhere, the *St Columba* is still a two-class vessel. Until recently…Irish workers returned home in droves and conditions could be fairly rough. The mix of passengers has fluctuated wildly in recent years and in 1970 about half were tourists. Since then, the combined effect of the troubles and the recession have reduced the total traffic by a fifth…many English people clearly decided that they did not want to spend their holidays among people with violent and hostile tendencies… Against such a background, it must have taken courage and optimism on the part of British Rail to order a ship which, together with associated terminal improvements, represents an investment of more than £20 million…"

Fortunately, the *St Columba* proved highly successful and, meanwhile, on the North Sea, the Harwich-Hook of Holland service – another two-class operation – was also booming, making a significant contribution to British Rail's Shipping and International Services Division's £8 million profit for 1978.

Another cause for optimism was the growth in duty-free shopping day-trips by coach and ferry across the Dover Strait, enabling passengers to stock up with cheap alcoholic drinks and cigarettes in French hypermarkets – a sign of an emerging new consumerism and that the mid-1970s recession was drawing to a close:

"Despite high winds and dampening rain…Sealink claimed a full complement of 1,400 on each sailing to Calais, Boulogne and Dieppe. Cross-Channel shopping has been described as Britain's fastest-growing leisure industry. But there was nothing leisurely about the assault on the continental hypermarket at Calais, a favourite destination with Sealink passengers. The queues at many of the hypermarket's 30 checkouts were composed entirely of British shoppers, comparing notes about prices, the intricacies of metric conversion and exchange rates… my straw poll among the pre-Christmas shoppers suggested that their total spending averaged £43, which would

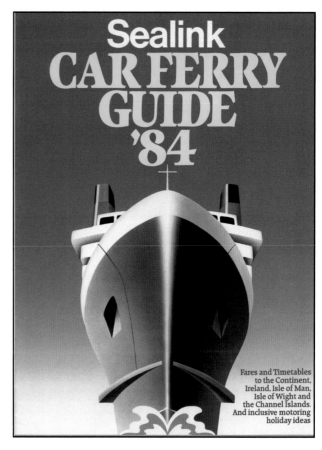

bring the cost of the day's total operations to almost precisely £500,000. It seems that the total haul would include 60,000 bottles of wine, 72,000 bottles of beer, 14,000 cheeses and 10,000 French loaves, besides an amazing variety of novelty nursery lamps, doll's chairs, and stew pots."

For increasing numbers of passengers, a ferry crossing provided an opportunity to imbibe large quantities of relatively cheap alcoholic drinks – and this occasionally created a raucous atmosphere – perhaps one of the consequences of increasing social mobility and the democratisation of international travel.

On 1st January 1979 the Shipping and International Services Division ceased to exist and its function, assets and staff were transferred to a new company wholly owned by the Board named Sealink UK Ltd. The setting up of Sealink UK Ltd, as a wholly owned subsidiary of the BRB, was exercised through the powers under Section 7 of the Transport Act 1968 through a scheme cited as the British Rail Shipping and Habour Scheme 1979.

Under the British Rail Shipping and Harbours Scheme 1979 the BRB also transferred to Sealink UK Ltd its interests in the following companies:

Passro (Shipping) Company Ltd
Passtruck (Shipping) Company Ltd
Sealink Ltd
Sealink Travel Ltd
Transport Ship Management (Scotland) Ltd
Fishguard and Rosslare Railways and Harbours Company (50%)
George Troy and Sons Ltd (44%)
Guernsey Stevedores Ltd (25%)
Société Anonyme de Navigation Angleterre-Lorraine-

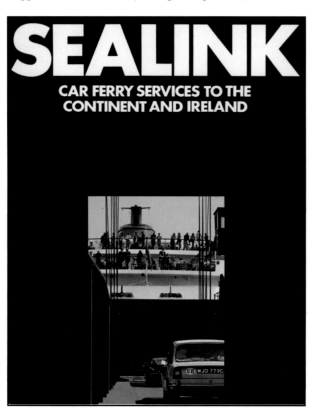

With a good load of containers, the cellular box boat *Sea Freightliner I* outward from Harwich. *(Don Smith/Phototransport.com)*

The *Earl William* at St Peter Port outward bound for Portsmouth. *(Ken Larwood)*

Dover-Calais Flagship Service! The *St Anselm* of 1980, before the extension of her accommodation aft and the opening of her top deck to increase passenger capacity. *(FotoFlite)*

The **Galloway Princess** on the Firth of Clyde during sea trials before entering service between Stranraer and Larne. (*AE Glen/Bruce Peter collection*)

Alsace
Société Belgo-Anglaise des Ferry Boats SA (13%)
Société Boulonnaise de Lamanage (1%)

In due course British Transport Ship Management (Scotland) Ltd became Sealink (Scotland) Ltd and Sealink UK Ltd subsequently acquired interests in:

Manx Line Holdings Ltd
Manx Line Ltd (100% of share capital held by Manx Line Holdings Ltd)

Sealink for Sale

On 14th July 1980 the British Transport Minister, Mr Norman Fowler, announced plans to denationalise the shipping, hovercraft and hotels sections of British Rail within the next two or three years. The injection of private capital, he said, into the non-rail subsidiaries, should allow them far more latitude although BR would be allowed to keep a minority shareholding in the businesses.

As Sealink was placed in the Conservative Government's shop window a group of consultants, H&P Associates, was hired to create a new image for the company whose ships carried the monastral blue, white and red livery for almost 20 years. Sealink's new corporate identity was launched on 27th March 1984 when the 17,000-tonne flagship *St Nicholas* unveiled the new look to an awaiting press at Dover. Managing Director Len Merryweather said the change of identity was not primarily conceived with privatisation in mind. "We are in a quality war and there has long been a need for a distinct change in our image without jeopardising investment in one of the best brand names in the business – a name which we intend carrying into the private sector," he said. The Times reported that:

"This big new 'funship' featuring discotheques, cabaret, saunas and a four-star restaurant has been hired by British Rail Sealink to pave the way for the line's sale to private industry later this year. [The ship will offer] a distinctly new style, including 24-

hour 'fun cruises' on Scandinavian lines with cheap drinks and quick shopping trips to Rotterdam and Amsterdam from £19 return from London. The profit will come largely from what people spend on board.

Sealink, which is under heavy pressure from the government to get on with 'privatising' the line in spite of £15 million losses over the past two years, hope the ship will increase traffic by half over the next five years and thus boost profits to make Sealink more attractive to investors. The £3 million annual rental is considered well worthwhile for a ship half as big again as any existing Sealink vessel which will replace two existing ships and cut operating costs by nearly half… The charter…has come after a year's conflict with unions, which ended in more than 200 redundancies."

Meanwhile, the British Railways Board invited tenders, through its advisers Morgan Grenfell and Co. Ltd for the purchase of the whole of the board's interest in Sealink UK Ltd. Three proposals were received with conditions attached. For a while it seemed a consortium of the National Freight Corporation, James Fisher & Sons Ltd and Sealink executives would win the day. However, on 24th July 1984 Sealink was sold to international sea freight company Sea Containers; paying £66 million for 37 ships of various size, ten harbours and 9,390 staff of whom 2,529 were salaried. For the acquisition a new Sea Containers subsidiary was formed; British Ferries Ltd.

The British Railways Board was advised that the price fairly reflected the value of the business. With assets valued at over £170 million, the Transport Minister stated that over the previous five years Sealink had lost, on average, £2.5 million a year. As a mixture of asset value and earnings ability, "the price of £66 million is a very reasonable one in the opinion of all the advisers and the Government," he said.

Thus Sealink UK Ltd became Sealink British Ferries Ltd. Initially at least, Sea Containers and its charismatic president James Sherwood, made a number of constructive proposals for improving Sealink's business. For many routes, new build tonnage was promised, but apart from the Isle of Wight services these failed to arrive.

Sealink
and before

CHAPTER TWO

North Sea

U pon nationalisation of the railways, the British Transport Commission inherited a wide variety of North Sea shipping services. Across the Humber, a fleet of ex-LNER paddle steamers operated where today there is an impressive suspension bridge. From Hull docks to Rotterdam, Associated Humber Lines ran a combined freight and passenger service.

But it was Harwich that was the centrepiece of North Sea routes to the continent. From there, train ferry and general cargo services ran to Zeebrugge, while passenger vessels operated jointly with the Dutch Stoomvaart Maatschappij Zeeland (SMZ, in English – The Zeeland Steamship Company) sailing from Parkeston Quay to the Hook of Holland. A passenger service also ran to Antwerp.

HOOK OF HOLLAND

British Railways' Harwich-Hook of Holland steamer service was the jewel in the crown of the Eastern Region, linking London with northern Europe's major cities and industrial regions. Most journeys began at London Liverpool Street, from which 'The Hook Continental' boat train ran directly to Parkeston Quay. In an era long before the advent of mass leisure travel, the vast majority of travellers across the North Sea in 1948 were business people, military personnel en route to barracks in an only recently liberated West Germany, plus some wealthy tourists.

The normal British Railways post-war routine was overnight crossings between Harwich and the Hook of Holland. These vessels sailed only eight out of every 24 hours, spending the remaining 16 hours tied up alongside – by latter-day standards a most inefficient way of running a ferry service. Daytime crossings from Harwich, on the other hand, were the exclusive domain of SMZ, ships of which also spent most of their existences tied up alongside.

The LNER's *Prague* reopened the civilian service from Harwich to the Hook of Holland on 14th November 1945 sailing on a thrice-weekly basis. She was joined by the SMZ steamer *Oranje Nassau*, a survivor of World War I that also came through the Second World War unscathed, before moving to the day service during the following year. Another survivor of the war was the *Mecklenberg* and she re-entered day services from Harwich in 1947. When the late 1930s vintage SMZ motor vessels *Koningin Emma* and *Prinses Beatrix* returned to service in 1948, the *Mecklenberg* introduced a new twice-weekly summer day service between Vlissingen (Flushing) and Folkestone in July 1949. Meanwhile the *Oranje Nassau* was chartered to Batavier Line for their Rotterdam-Tilbury service.

In addition to the regular service British troops were carried in large numbers on two dedicated vessels, the *Vienna* and the *Empire Parkeston*, the former being an ex-LNER steamer while the latter was originally built for North American coastal service.

Just as the route was pulling itself together after the war a major setback was suffered when in March 1948 fire broke out in the engine room of the refitting *Prague*. Heeling over and coming to rest on the dry dock wall, the blaze left the ship only fit for the scrap yard. The replacement vessel was the *Duke of York* of 1935 which was transferred from the Heysham to Belfast crossing to take up service in May 1948.

The initial removal of the *Duke of York* from Heysham met with some protest in Northern Ireland and gave cause for Sir

months to complete and, in the interim British Railways chartered the redundant *Oranje Nassau*; a swansong for the veteran ship before meeting her fate in a breakers yard the following year. During spring of 1954 the *Arnhem* was converted to a two-class vessel.

In the early 1960s, both British Railways and SMZ responded to an expanding overseas travel market by each commissioning an additional vessel. While the Dutch commissioned a further motor ship with limited car capacity, the *Koningin Wilhelmina*, BR ordered yet another turbine steamer as a replacement for the *Duke of York*. The contract was won by the Clyde shipyard of Alexander Stephen & Sons of Linthouse. Delivered in 1963 the *Avalon* was highly regarded for her interior design and general level of comfort – indeed, she was frequently used out of season as a cruise ship, bringing the newly affluent middle class on itineraries to Baltic ports, the Western Mediterranean and even North Africa. Still, as she was unable to carry vehicles – notwithstanding a great growth in car ownership – this rendered her obsolete almost from the outset.

LATE CAR FERRY EMBRACE

In 1966, a Swedish ferry entrepreneur, Lion Ferry, which was owned by the Bonnier publishing company, began a car ferry route from Harwich to Bremerhaven in West Germany and this provided a powerful challenge to British Rail (as it by then was renamed) and SMZ on the Harwich-Hook of Holland crossing. The best solution was for each to build a car ferry and for these vessels to provide both morning and evening departures, supplemented by the *Avalon* and *Koningin Wilhelmina* – after all, the vast majority of passengers would still arrive by rail at each port and so it remained desirable to maintain a large capacity.

At first, BR and SMZ proposed ferries of entirely different design, but soon the Dutch sensibly decided that it would be wiser to use the layout of the Swan Hunter-built British vessel, the *St George*, as a basis for the design of their *Koningin Juliana*; thus, both vessels ended up having a similar general

The LNER overnight steamer ***Vienna*** operated between Harwich Parkeston Quay and Hook of Holland from 1929 until the Second World War. She was never returned to civilian service and operated in the post-war era as a troop transporter. *(Jim Ashby collection)*

Ronald Ross MP for Londonderry to raise the subject in the House of Commons on 1st December 1949.

"With regard to ships, one of the ships, the *Duke of York*, from the Heysham service has been moved round to the Harwich service. This vessel used to give a Sunday night service. If I have a meeting on Saturday night now and wish to travel by sea and rail I cannot get to this House on Monday. If anything goes wrong on the Harwich service, if a ship has to have her boilers attended to, they have to take one off the Heysham service and send it round."

The *Duke of York* joined the *Arnhem*, completed in 1947 and named after the town where in September 1944 the 1st Airborne Division resisted the German Army. The design of the new ship was basically pre-war, although built with a single funnel and, in order to pick up the cruise market once again, she was fitted out as a one-class steamer.

A new near-sister to the *Arnhem* was launched at John Brown's Clydebank yard on 19th January 1950. The magnificent *Amsterdam* arrived at Harwich on 29th May under the command of Captain C.R. Baxter, the third vessel to carry the name. While the Dutch daytime vessels could carry a small number of cars, loaded through side doors, British Railways' overnight vessels were pure passenger ships, in style rather like miniaturised versions of ocean liners of their era (and likewise built by John Brown & Co. of Clydebank). First Class passengers experienced expanses of polished marquetry, a dining saloon with a ceiling dome and the near silence of turbine propulsion.

On 6th May 1953 the *Duke of York* collided off Harwich with an American freighter, the *Haiti Victory*, severing her bow, which sank, killing eight. As her watertight bulkheads were closed, her mid-body and stern remained afloat and she was towed stern-first back to port. Repairs on the Tyne took no less than ten

The ex-Irish Sea steamer ***Duke of York*** (built in Belfast in 1935) was switched to the Harwich-Hook of Holland route after the Second World War. In May 1953, she collided with a US-flagged cargo ship, the ***Haiti Victory***, which sheared off the steamer's bow, killing six of her passengers. Here, the seriously damaged vessel is seen back at Harwich. Rebuilding work lasted into the following year and the ***Duke of York*** continued on the route until 1963, when sold to Greek interests. *(Jim Ashby collection)*

The BR (ex LNER) overnight turbine steamer *Arnhem* manoeuvres off the berth at Hook of Holland with the oil storages of Europort in the background. *(Bruce Peter collection)*

arrangement and capacity, making the service operationally straightforward. The *Koningin Juliana* was, however, built by Cammell Laird at Birkenhead on the River Mersey.

In anticipation of the appearance of the *St George*, the *Arnhem* sailed from the Hook of Holland for the last time on the evening of 27th April 1968. Arriving at Harwich the next morning, she discharged and went to lay up pending sale. Her master, Captain Clifford Witchell, retired at the same time. Sold for scrap, she was at the Inverkeithing yard of T. W. Ward Ltd in August 1968.

The new ferry service was a great success – but each of the two vessels had teething problems; the *St George* suffering acute vibrations towards her stern (where First Class berths were located) and the *Koningin Juliana* needing a new bow visor with a less pronounced flair so as not to catch high waves, which strained the locking pins.

To the sound of salutes from the whistles of nearby ships, the *Amsterdam* left Harwich for the last time on 1st May 1969 bound for the Greek port of Piraeus. Sold to Chandris she was destined to join the *Fantasia*, ex-*Duke of York*, running cruises around the Mediterranean.

As the travel market was growing overall, in 1972 British Rail ordered a further vessel for the route. As with the *Koningin Juliana*, she was constructed by Cammell Laird and delivered in 1974 as the *St Edmund*. The pride of the BR fleet, her well-

appointed passenger accommodation, particularly in First Class, soon won praise from regular travellers. In the interval between ordering and taking delivery, however, the price of oil quadrupled due to Arab OPEC nations protesting against western support for Israel in the Yom Kippur war. Although the *St Edmund* was a costly investment, as a diesel ship, she was much more economical to operate than the *Avalon*, which was displaced for further service on the Irish Sea.

By now the Hook of Holland route had gained direct competition for motorists and freight hauliers from a new service inaugurated by the Danish-owned Olau Line, linking Sheerness in the Thames estuary with Vlissingen in the Netherlands. Although Olau began in 1974 with one small freight ferry, by the mid-1970s, two much larger vessels were being used.

Four years after the arrival of the *St Edmund* SMZ introduced a fourth drive-through car ferry, the *Prinses Beatrix*, built by Verolme Scheepswerf Heusden in the Netherlands. She was the biggest vessel yet seen on the route – but was soon eclipsed by two significantly larger vessels introduced by Olau Line in 1981 – the *Olau Hollandia* and *Olau Britannia*.

Substantial losses were mounting on the Hook of Holland service and if it was to survive then Sealink had to take corrective action. In an effort to recover economic viability on this service, Sealink sought to establish new manning arrangements for both officers and crew on the *St Edmund* and

The **Essex Ferry**, built at Clydebank in 1957, was one of a series of diesel-powered train ferries operating from Harwich Town to Zeebrugge. Here, the vessel is shown at Parkeston Quay in the early 1960s. The train ferries carried freight and were known for their 'lively' motion in the North Sea swells. *(Bruce Peter collection)*

the *St George*.

With the increased competition from Olau, Sealink looked at the possibility of a bigger, more efficient ship being introduced on to the route to replace the two older and smaller ships. Their opportunity came remarkably quickly.

The invasion of the Falklands Islands by Argentina in the spring of 1982 led to the British Government requisitioning a broad cross-section of the UK-flagged merchant fleet to act as supply ships and troop transports. One of the vessels called up was the eight year old *St Edmund*. To fill the gap, the Danish-owned, but West German-flagged *Prinz Oberon* was chartered as a stop-gap measure.

In Sweden, meanwhile, two rival ferry operators on routes between Sweden, Denmark and West Germany across the Kattegat, Stena Line and Sessanlinjen, had each ordered a pair of unprecedentedly large jumbo ferries for the three and a half hour crossing between Gothenburg and Frederikshavn. As there was insufficient custom to fill so much capacity throughout the year, the companies' financiers began to fret about these high-risk and costly investments. Stena, which in recent years had a better record for profitability, was therefore encouraged to take over Sessan, which was having difficulties in raising enough capital to complete the second of its two 17,043gt vessels, under construction at the Gothenburg Arendal Shipyard. As Stena's own jumbo ferries were delayed at their builder in France, the first of Sessan's twins therefore entered service as

The recently delivered turbine steamer **Avalon**, operating the night service to Hook of Holland, at Harwich Parkeston Quay in the early 1960s. *(Bruce Peter collection)*

planned, but under Stena's ownership. Meanwhile, work was temporarily suspended on the second vessel, which was eventually completed in 1982 as the *Prinsessan Birgitta*. Towards the end of her maiden season on the Gothenburg-Frederikshavn route, Stena entered negotiations with Sealink to charter her for Harwich-Hook of Holland service, replacing both the *St George* and the *Prinz Oberon*.

When the British seafarers' unions discovered what was being planned, they were furious at the idea of two relatively labour-intensive ships being superseded by one more efficient vessel, but in the end, they conceded. Although intended primarily as a daytime ferry, the *Prinsessan Birgitta* nonetheless had 616 cabin berths, Sessanlinjen's original intention having been to offer overnight mini-cruises. As this capacity was insufficient for night crossings of the North Sea, the vessel's upper vehicle deck was converted with additional cabins and

painted in the new blue and yellow livery in which the Sealink UK fleet entered the private sector. Of course, the *St Nicholas* could offer a very different kind of travel experience from the *Koningin Juliana* and *Prinses Beatrix*. As a stop-gap measure, SMZ chartered the Norwegian ferry *Peter Wessel* as a replacement for the *Koningin Juliana* between 1984 and 1986, pending the construction of a new jumbo ferry, the *Koningin Beatrix*, which entered service in April 1986.

In 1989, SMZ was acquired by Stena Line and in 1990 Stena bought Sealink British Ferries, thus for the first time, the Dutch and British operations were under the same ownership.

ROTTERDAM, ANTWERP, ZEEBRUGGE AND DUNKIRK

After the war the Harwich-Zeebrugge train ferry service was reopened by the *Essex Ferry*, originally the LNER's *Train Ferry*

At twilight, a caravan is loaded by crane onto the **Avalon**'s aft deck; this time-consuming and precarious-looking approach to loading vehicles demonstrates the clear need for a ro-ro service – but British Railways was much more keen to serve foot passengers arriving by rail. *(Jim Ashby collection)*

This BR publicity image lends the night service to Hook of Holland a romantic allure as passengers are welcomed at the foot of the **Avalon**'s gangway. In driving rain or the freezing fog of winter, it would have been far less pleasant and a world away from the fully enclosed access walkways in use today. *(Bruce Peter collection)*

reclining seat saloons installed in containers, none of which had any windows. This work boosted capacity to 1,100 berths. The *Prinsessan Birgitta* was, of course, a one-class ship and her main entertainment space was a very large, tiered show lounge, located towards the stern, which did not lend itself to any form of subdivision. Sealink decided that the à la carte restaurant and a small aft-facing cocktail lounge would constitute the vessel's First Class accommodation, meaning that the vast majority of the ship would be available to all passengers.

In June 1983, the ship entered service as the *St Nicholas* and her impact was immediate, a significant boost in patronage being recorded. By this point, Sealink UK was up for sale and so the British rail 'double arrow' logo never was applied to her funnel. Soon, she became the first member of the fleet to be

No.1. Built for the service in 1919 she was purchased by the Admiralty in late June 1940 and converted to a Landing Ship capable of carrying 14 landing craft in the train deck. Commissioned as HMS *Iris* in April 1941, changing to HMS *Princess Iris* in September 1942, she spent most of her time ferrying landing craft to southern ports. After the Normandy invasion, she ferried damaged craft back to the UK. In August 1944 she was re-converted to carry locomotives from Southampton to Cherbourg and Dieppe, but by 1945 she was again ferrying landing craft, until released in May 1946 when she was re-sold to the LNER as the *Essex Ferry*.

The *Suffolk Ferry* came along in August 1947 and was the first diesel-powered ship built for the LNER. She was followed in July 1951 by the *Norfolk Ferry* and in 1957 a new *Essex Ferry*

The **Amsterdam** and **Avalon** at Harwich Parkeston Quay. *(FototFlite)*

replaced her predecessor of the same name which was broken up later that year.

While the train ferries carried rail traffic to and from Zeebrugge, general cargo was conveyed to Rotterdam and Antwerp in the *Isle of Ely* and the *Colchester*, built at Goole and delivered in 1958-59 to replace the elderly pair *Sheringham* and the *Dewsbury* respectively.

The *Dewsbury* had reopened the Antwerp service alongside the *Accrington* in 1946, however, passenger numbers were in decline and in 1949 it was decided to cease the passenger element of the route. The last passenger sailing was taken by the *Dewsbury* on 3rd February 1950 but such was the outcry that by July the ship was offering accommodation for up to 12 passengers.

A further new train ferry was ordered from Hawthorn Leslie, Hebburn in 1962. Built at a cost of £700,000, the *Cambridge Ferry* was completed in December 1963 and on 2nd January she made her maiden voyage from Harwich to Zeebrugge.

In March 1968 British Rail launched the 'Sea Link' in its Freightliner ISO container services. With purpose-built cellular container ships, the first of their kind to be built in Britain, and dedicated terminals, the Harwich-Zeebrugge service was showcased as the future of sea-borne cargo transportation. The first of the two new container ships *Sea Freightliner I* entered service on 17th March 1968 and was in June followed by the *Sea Freightliner II*. The arrival of the latter saw the closure of the Antwerp route and the opening of a second container service from Harwich to Rotterdam, operated jointly with SMZ who contributed the *Domburgh* to sail alongside the *Colchester*. This, however, failed to perform and the Rotterdam link was eventually closed in 1973.

During 1967 British Rail launched a new train ferry service between Harwich and Dunkirk using the *Norfolk Ferry* and two years later SNCF appeared on the link with the container/ro-ro ship *Transcontainer I*. Holyhead's *Rhodri Mawr* also appeared in service in 1975. In 1977 the *Cambridge Ferry* was extended at a cost of £91,000 to enable her to carry an additional 50 trade cars, and also to use the docks at Dunkirk.

Cost cuts brought the withdrawal of the *Suffolk Ferry* from service in September 1980, followed by the *Norfolk Ferry* and the *Essex Ferry* in 1981. With the *Cambridge Ferry* now designated as reserve ship the Zeebrugge service was in the hands of the chartered *Speedlink Vanguard*.

Unlike most of Sealink's other services, the train ferries were paid for by British Rail's rail freight business, Freightliner. On the

train ferries, Sealink was very much in an agency role. The freight business had hoped to build up the service to a point where investment in new jumbo train ferries would be possible. These would be much larger than the existing ships and would offer a better and more efficient service. The government gave approval to the project, subject to the obvious proviso that the investment should be made on an economically viable basis. The *Speedlink Vanguard* had been chartered so that she could begin to build up traffic to a level that would require the jumbo ferries. In terms of traffic levels this was well on the way to that objective. However, the revenue that the service was generating in a highly competitive environment with competition from the ro-ro sector was insufficient to make it a paying proposition.

Keeping a sharp lookout, the Master on the bridge of the **Cambridge Ferry**. *(Jim Ashby collection)*

Arnhem

The launching of the **Arnhem** at John Brown & Co's Clydebank shipyard on 30th October 1946. The steam turbine-driven overnight vessel was delivered to the LNER, whereas her near-sister, the **Amsterdam** of 1950 joined the recently created British Railways fleet. Intriguingly, the vessels' midships hull and machinery design was re-used by the yard's drawing office for the Royal Yacht **Britannia**. (Bruce Peter collection)

Left: Inboard, the **Arnhem** and **Amsterdam** were outfitted in the manner of late 1930s 'deep sea' ocean liners with polished veneers with polished metal inlays and 'streamlined' or 'Art Deco' details by these finishes were supplemented by the typically floral upholstery and curtains of railway steamers of an even earlier era. Here, we see the **Arnhem**'s First Class saloon, the intention being (presumably) to resonate with a broad range of popular taste. (Bruce Peter collection)

Above: A First Class cabin on the **Arnhem**, almost entirely lined in polished bird's eye maple and with shiny silk bed linen; had one not known that this space was on an overnight packet vessel, one might have assumed that it was on one of the trans-Atlantic liners produced by the same shipbuilder. (Bruce Peter collection)

Loading of a special wagon for Yugosalvia on board the **Suffolk Ferry** at Harwich. *(Jim Ashby collection)*

With the arrangements for sharing revenue with the European railways, British Rail's prospect of a jumbo ferry service that could achieve viability slipped away. Once this conclusion had been reached management could not allow the existing losses to continue unabated and withdrew the service to Dunkirk, which was also served from the BR system by the

Dover-Dunkirk route.

The end finally came when the *Cambridge Ferry* was withdrawn on Christmas Eve 1986 and the *Speedlink Vanguard* left Harwich for the last time on 29th January 1987.

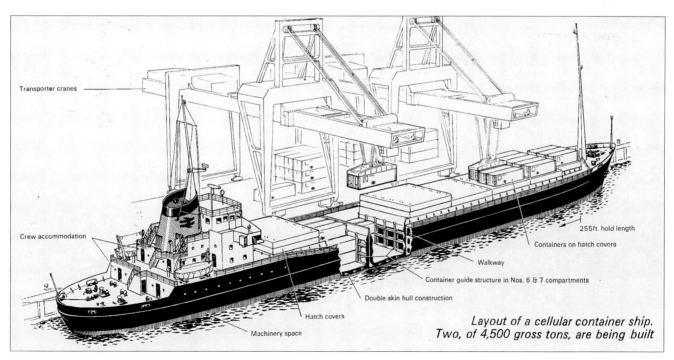

A British Rail concept drawing for a cellular container ship. *(Bruce Peter collection)*

Avalon

Upon entering service in 1963, the **Avalon** brought a new and radically different aesthetic to British Railways' North Sea fleet. The vessel's interior design by Ward & Austin was highly praised for its elegance and functionality with up-to-date 'wipe clean' surfaces predominating throughout. Here, we see the forward part of the vessel's First Class smoking saloon. *(Bruce Peter collection)*

Top right: The same space, looking aft and to starboard, showing the bar counter, which made extensive use of brushed aluminium. Beneath the bar is a trough to catch cigarette ash and butts, it being an important and well-established British cultural tradition when drinking to drop these items, rather than to use an ash tray on the bar counter. *(Bruce Peter collection)*

Centre right: A spacious First Class cabin on the **Avalon**, finished in matt veneers and with a rather less ostentatious (and arguably more appropriate) design style than was found on the route's existing overnight vessels. The fact that the models are smoking in bed is intriguing and today – quite rightly – would cause a ferry's safety officer the gravest concern. Back in the 1960s, smokers presumed the right to 'light up' almost anywhere. *(Bruce Peter collection)*

Right: The **Avalon**'s First Class dining saloon was the only space on the vessel with wood veneer bulkhead finishes, creating a cosy atmosphere perhaps inspired by the design of the interiors of Scandinavian passenger ships of the same era, design from Denmark and Sweden being much admired and emulated in the UK. *(Bruce Peter collection)*

Left: Seen tied up at a mooring buoy in the River Stour off Harwich in the latter 1960s, the 1951-built Harwich-Zeebrugge train ferry *Norfolk Ferry* was, like the Hook of Holland route passenger ships, a product of John Brown & Co. of Clydebank. *(FotoFlite)*

Below left: A mix of trade cars and rail freight on the *Suffolk Ferry*. *(Jim Ashby collection)*

Below: Loading the *Suffolk Ferry* at Harwich. *((Jim Ashby collection)*

Bottom left: The *Suffolk Ferry* at rest on the buoys in the River Stour. *(Jim Ashby collection)*

Above: The 1963-built *Cambridge Ferry*, a product of Hawthorn Leslie & Co. on the Tyne, is seen 'on the buoys' off Harwich in the mid-1970s. *(Ken Larwood)*

Left: A 1950s view of the general cargo vessel *Colchester* loading freight at Harwich with the troopship *Vienna* in the background. *(Jim Ashby collection)*

Below: The final train ferry on the Harwich-Zeebrugge route was the *Speedlink Vanguard*, a vessel built in The Netherlands in 1973 for Stena and chartered by British Rail from 1980 until early 1987 when the route was closed. *(Miles Cowsill)*

The **Sea Freightliner II** at Harwich awaiting cargo for transport. *(Jim Ashby collection)*

The container vessel **Sea Freightliner II**. *(Jim Ashby collection)*

St George

Above: The First Class bar and smoking saloon on the 1968 Harwich-Hook of Holland ferry **St George**, designed by Ward Associates (formerly Ward & Austin) was an attempt to replicate the success of the similarly laid out facility on the **Avalon**. In this instance, a 'floating' timber-clad ceiling soffit was installed and greater use was made of timber veneers to engender a warm and welcoming atmosphere. Part of the vessel's First Class dining saloon can be glimpsed through the plate glass doors on the left. *(Bruce Peter collection)*

Centre: The oval-shaped Second Class saloon was aft-located and finished in Formica laminates, giving a slightly space-age character. The **St George** was, however, plagued by vibration and so the futuristic styling would doubtless have been accompanied by constant rattling. *(Bruce Peter collection)*

Below: The First Class hallway and kiosk, amidships on the **St George**'s Main deck, had vertical mirrors on the outer wall panelling to give an illusion of greater width. *(Bruce Peter collection)*

St Edmund

Left: The **St Edmund** of 1974 was one of the most strikingly decorated of the British Rail ferry fleet – but also among the shortest to serve Sealink, lasting on the Harwich-Hook of Holland route only until the 1982 Falklands War. Here, we see the midships section of the vessel's First Class lounge, designed by Ward Associates and featuring a glassfibre bas relief panel depicting in abstract form the martyrdom of Edmund, after whom the vessel was named. *(Bruce Peter collection)*

Below left: The forward bulkhead of the **St Edmund**'s Second Class bar, panelled in bright red Formica, a material used concurrently ashore in great quantity by British Rail's Traveller's Fare subsidiary. Indeed, the space appears rather as a shipboard rendition of one of the better-designed station buffet bars of the same era. The seats are plastic and bolted to the linoleum floor. *(Bruce Peter collection)*

Below: The **St Edmund**'s most impressive space was the hallway amidships on the Main Deck, which featured five circular inter-connecting spaces with glassfibre 'trumpet' columns and peripheral banquet seating, each rendered in a different bright colour. The vessel was introduced at a time when British Rail was developing the Inter-City 125 and the Advanced Passenger Train and so the 'future' was imagined in terms of jet and space age imagery that was actually most convincingly achievable in the more spacious surroundings of a ship. *(Bruce Peter collection)*

Above: The *St Edmund* is seen off Harwich in the latter 1970s, apparently heavily loaded with passengers, who are lining the deck railings around the superstructure. *(Bruce Peter collection)*

Left: The *St George* is seen crossing the North Sea in the mid-1970s. The vessel was Tyne-built by Swan Hunter and served until 1982 when laid up prior to sale to Greek interests. For a ship intended to make day and night sailings, the superstructure has very few windows and the vast majority of cabins were 'insides'. *(Ken Larwood)*

Below: The *Avalon* dressed overall during one of her spring cruises, prior to her conversion to a car ferry for the Irish Sea. *(Captain Walter Lloyd Williams)*

The troop transporter and military supplies vessel **Keren** (ex-**St Edmund**) as she appeared in the years following the Falklands War. *(FotoFlite)*

A stern-quarter view of the jumbo ferry **St Nicholas**. *(FotoFlite)*

English Channel and the Channel Islands

DOVER & FOLKESTONE

WORLD WAR II

On the last day of the Southern Railway Company, 31st December 1947, the combined Dover and Folkestone fleets were still in the process of adjusting from the effects of the Second World War. Losses during this period had been significant and of those vessels which had survived, much rebuilding and refurbishment was required in order to bring them back into civilian service.

The hospital ship *Maid of Kent* (1925) had been bombed and burnt out whilst alongside in the inner harbour of Dieppe in May 1940 whilst the *Maid of Orleans* (1918) was sunk when returning empty from the Normandy beaches in June 1944. Of the then important cargo ship fleet, the *Tonbridge* was bombed and sunk whilst acting as a net layer off Great Yarmouth in August 1941 although her sisters *Hythe*, *Whitstable, Maidstone* and *Deal* all survived.

An immediate order for a replacement for the lost passenger steamers was made and the second *Maid of Orleans* was launched at Denny's Dumbarton yard in September 1948, becoming the first local ship to enter service for the nationalised railway company.

The rest of the fleet comprised the passenger steamers *Isle of Thanet* (1925), *Canterbury* (1929) and the new 'Golden Arrow' vessel *Invicta* (1940) which was launched after war had broken out. In addition to the passenger fleet, the lift on-lift off car ferry *Autocarrier* (1931) and the train ferries *Shepperton Ferry* and *Hampton Ferry* (1935) had also survived as had their French-flagged sister ship *Twickenham Ferry*. One further ship was the *Biarritz* (1915) which had been built for the South Eastern & Chatham Railway and was the only local ship to serve in both world wars. Due to her age and condition, she was due for replacement and operated her final post-war years trooping for the Ministry of Transport. Thus, although technically she was owned by the British Transport Commission, she did not operate for them and was scrapped on the foreshore at Dover's Eastern Docks in 1949.

RESTARTING THE BUSINESS

With Dover Harbour in use by the Admiralty until November 1946, post-war services started from Folkestone with a cargo service to Calais commencing as early as August 1945 using the sister ships *Maidstone* and *Hythe*. At the end of October the *Canterbury* reappeared on the same route prior to retiring to the Tyne for a well-earned refit. In March 1946 the Folkestone-Boulogne cargo service was reinstated whilst the *Isle of Thanet* was back on station in January 1947, reopening the Dover-Boulogne service in July and the service from Folkestone in June of the following year. Resplendent from overhaul the *Canterbury* reopened the Dover-Calais 'Golden Arrow' service in April 1946 before the *Invicta* replaced her in October.

The train ferry service linking Dover and Dunkirk eventually recommenced in November 1947. Towards the end of the war, the three ferries had huge gantries fitted at their after ends in order that they could offload heavy military equipment and locomotives at French ports which had been so badly damaged that it would have been impossible to disembark it via conventional methods.

NATIONALISATION

Nationalisation on New Year's Day 1948 was a fairly

Above: The *Deal* was the final vessel of a series of nine sister ships which were built by D&W Henderson at Partick (Glasgow) between 1924 and 1928. She is seen alongside the *Isle of Thanet* in Dover's Wellington Dock following her withdrawal from service in March 1963. *(Michael Woodland)*

Left: The former 'Golden Arrow' steamer *Canterbury* is seen relieving on her original Dover-Calais service as she glides across Dover Harbour inward bound in May 1960. *(Henry Maxwell/ John Hendy collection)*

Below: The end of an era as, dressed overall, the *Isle of Thanet* arrives in the Wellington Dock at Dover to lay up pending sale on 16th September 1963. *(Mark Leiper collection)*

Throughout the British Railways era, the ships of the Dover and Folkestone fleets would take turns to enter Dover's Wellington Dock to undergo their annual refits by personnel from the local Packet Yard - a name steeped in history. The **Hengist** and the **Horsa** were the largest vessels to use this facility but the later 'Saint' class were too large to enter the port's inner docks and so sights such as this became more infrequent with the passing of time. This image dates from October 1958 showing the Folkestone - Boulogne excursion vessel *Isle of Thanet* in the company of the 'Golden Arrow' steamer *Invicta*. *(Henry Maxwell/ John Hendy collection)*

The converted passenger steamer **Normannia** took up sailings between Dover and Boulogne in April 1964. *(John Hendy)*

seamless occasion, a new BR house flag eventually being the only outward sign of change. The entry into service at Folkestone of the new *Maid of Orleans* in June 1949 was the cause for much celebration but the post-war link to Boulogne was now a seasonal affair while the port's new Calais service continued to run year-round.

Two of the main features of the Short-Sea routes during the immediate post-war years were a) the continuing increase in tourist motor vehicle traffic and b) the resurgence of the

nationalised French railway company SNCF who in 1951 introduced the train ferry *Saint-Germain* on the Dunkirk crossing and the turbine passenger steamer *Cote d'Azur* on the Calais-Folkestone link. What had hitherto been the preserve of British-crewed ships caused a degree of local consternation as SNCF gained a 25 per cent share in the train ferry route (by the time of its eventual closure they held a monopoly) while the *Cote d'Azur*'s daily crossing was at the expense of a BR vessel. With the Folkestone-Boulogne route closed during the winter

The 'Golden Arrow' steamer **Invicta** was a single route ship, operating the daily Dover-Calais service from 1946 until her withdrawal in August 1972 after which she was replaced in the fleet by the **Horsa**. *(Ken Larwood)*

The through London-Paris 'Night Ferry' service was introduced by the Southern Railway in October 1936 and continued until its withdrawal in October 1980. Carriages to/ from Brussels were added in 1957. *(Bruce Peter collection)*

months, the *Maid of Orleans*, *Canterbury* and *Isle of Thanet* all took their turns at relieving the *Invicta* and *Cote d'Azur* during their annual overhauls and were at times required to run what were called 'agents specials' which could be anything from parties of pilgrims visiting the Holy Shrines at Lourdes or Lisieux, to winter ski-groups. Otherwise they were laid up in the Wellington or Granville Docks at Dover.

In May 1946, the lift on-lift off (lo-lo) car ferry *Autocarrier* (1931) had reinstated her Dover-Calais service but at the end of March 1947 she was transferred to the Folkestone-Boulogne route. In her place came the former overnight steamer *Dinard* which had been built in 1924 for the Southampton-St Malo link. At the war's end she was sent to the Tyne and converted into a car ferry accommodating 361 passengers and 70 cars. The ship duly opened a new seasonal service from Dover to Boulogne's Bassin Loubet in July 1947 from where she continued to operate until the port's new car ferry terminal was opened in May 1952. In preparation for this, and also the opening of Dover's new car ferry terminal at the Eastern Docks in June 1953, she was sent to Falmouth in 1952 and re-emerged as a drive on-drive off ferry. The *Autocarrier*, meanwhile, served out the remainder of her career in a fairly peripatetic role, even running on the Southampton-St Malo link in 1949 before settling down on the Folkestone-Calais crossing on which she remained until her withdrawal from service and breaking in 1954. During her 1949 absence, BR had chartered the elderly Belgian Marine car ferry *London Istanbul* (ex *Ville de Liege* of 1913) to operate the Folkestone-Calais car ferry service and when she failed with boiler troubles in September, the new cargo vessel *Winchester* was brought up from Southampton until the end of the season in early October. During this unsatisfactory period, all motorists were taken by coach to Dover to join the *Invicta* while their cars were shipped to Calais

where they were later reunited.

Of the other cargo steamers, the *Maidstone* was transferred to Heysham in 1953 while the *Hythe* and *Whitstable* were moved to Southampton to replace war losses leaving just the *Deal* to operate the Folkestone-Boulogne tidal cargo service from the port's old Outer Harbour.

England's first purpose-built cross-Channel car ferry joined the fleet in June 1952. The seasonal service to Boulogne was scheduled to operate between April and October and on the occasion of the entry into service of the new Denny-built *Lord Warden* (120 cars, 1,000 passengers), the *Dinard* stood down but was scheduled to operate an additional sailing on Wednesdays, Thursdays and Fridays. Prior to the Eastern Docks car ferry terminal being opened, the *Dinard* and *Lord Warden* operated from berth 1 on Dover's Admiralty Pier from where cars were loaded in the time-honoured lift on-lift off method. Unfortunately, within a month of entering service, the new ship developed turbine problems as a result of which she retired to Southampton for attention. In her place both the *Dinard* and the train ferry *Hampton Ferry* were called in to deputise, the latter at weekends.

The tragic loss of the Stranraer-Larne car ferry *Princess Victoria* in January 1953 saw the *Hampton Ferry* transferred to Scotland for subsequent summer seasons until such time that the *Caledonian Princess* entered service as her replacement.

Such was the summer weekend demand for passenger space on the Southampton-Guernsey link that in 1949 and between 1952 and 1958, the *Isle of Thanet* sailed westward and was employed on an overnight sailing, returning to Southampton on the following day. Ever since the war's end, there had been calls to reinstate no-passport day excursions between Folkestone and Boulogne. These were finally started on weekdays in June 1955 using the normal service steamer but on Wednesdays during the peak season the *Isle of Thanet* was rostered to operate as a dedicated excursion ship. In 1956, some 80,000 day trippers took advantage of the sailings.

During October 1952, the legendary 'Golden Arrow' service was diverted via Folkestone-Calais on its outward run to enable SNCF to operate just one train and therefore make considerable savings. This arrangement lasted until May 1960 when once again both inward and outward sailings passed through Dover Marine.

Such was the demand for car ferry bookings that in September 1955 the order for a large replacement vessel for the *Dinard* was made at Denny's Dumbarton yard. It was to be their final ship for the local railway fleet; a link that had stretched back to 1896 when the London Chatham & Dover Railway had provided the paddle steamers *Dover*, *Calais* and *Lord Warden*.

The new *Maid of Kent* (known in the press as 'Dover's mini liner') finally entered service in May 1959 allowing the 35 year old *Dinard* to be sold to Viking Line where she kick-started the vehicle ferry revolution in the Baltic. Renamed *Viking*, the ship was not broken up until 1974 – her 50th year. The *Maid of Kent* carried as many as 180 cars, the construction of internal mezzanine decks allowing for the increase in capacity over the earlier *Lord Warden*. And yet, the success of the Dover-Boulogne car ferry continued apace frequently necessitating the use of a spare train ferry at peak summer weekends. Even with the addition of the new SNCF car ferry *Compiegne*, which entered service on the Calais-Dover link during 1958, demand frequently outstripped available capacity.

Fortunately assistance was at hand from Southampton where BR had for many years been looking to close their overnight services to Le Havre and St Malo. Permission was finally given during 1963 and the two spare ships – the *Normannia* and *Falaise* – were converted to car ferries for Dover and Newhaven. The *Normannia* arrived at Dover from the Tyne during April 1964 and although of limited capacity in her new role (500 passengers, 111 cars), certainly alleviated the problems that Dover was at that time experiencing.

FOLKESTONE

The end of a significant era was reached when at the end of the 1963 summer season, the *Isle of Thanet* was finally retired from service. Towards the end, her engineers had struggled to keep her operational but she was given a rousing send off and flew a 38 foot long pennant from her main mast – a foot for every year in service. Her Master and crew joined the 'new' *Normannia* and the Folkestone-Boulogne service was down to two ships. Worse was to follow as in September 1964, the former 'Golden Arrow' steamer *Canterbury* quietly bowed out and before the end of the year was replaced by the former Great Western Railway steamer *St Patrick* which was no longer required on the Weymouth-Channel Islands service.

The new British Rail livery was first seen at Dover in October 1964 when the *Lord Warden* was thus painted whilst undergoing her annual refit in the Wellington Dock. On the opposite side of the dock, the condemned *Canterbury* proudly retained her black hull and buff, black-topped funnel – the last link with the 1920s and a livery which was unsurpassed.

The *St Patrick* and the *Maid of Orleans* were to maintain the seasonal Folkestone-Boulogne passenger service until it was eventually converted to car ferry use in July 1972. The *St Patrick* finished her service at the close of the 1971 season before sailing to Greece for further work.

The long established Folkestone-Boulogne cargo link was also a casualty of the sixties. Specially constructed 'merchandise steamers' had been introduced by the South Eastern Railway in 1878 and it is interesting that every subsequent such ship was screw driven although the route's early paddle steamers had served out their days carrying cargo. The very last of the series of nine coal burning sister ships built by D & W Henderson of Glasgow for the Southern Railway between 1924 and 1928 was the *Deal* which finally finished service in March 1963. Her place was taken by the chartered Coast Line's vessel *Dorset Coast* which, in turn, was replaced during September 1965 by Associated Humber Line's *Darlington* before the *Winchester* and finally the Dieppe cargo vessel *Brest* arrived. The historic service eventually closed at the end of November 1966.

FURTHER CAR FERRIES AND A SWITCH TO CALAIS

A fourth car ferry for the Dover-Boulogne service was introduced during June 1965. This was the *Dover* which was built on the Tyne by Swan Hunter and which carried as many as 205 cars. With SNCF also introducing new tonnage on their Calais-Dover link during 1966, the combined railway fleets operated as 'The Big Fleet'.

Ever sensitive to the growing swell of criticism concerning the age of its fleet, and especially the state and facilities of the three original train ferries, British Rail ordered the revolutionary *Vortigern* from Swan Hunter's on the Tyne. She was to replace the *Hampton Ferry* on the Dunkirk route and the elderly ship was downgraded to freight workings with just two lifeboats before retiring to Holyhead to await disposal.

The *Vortigern* was the first local railway-owned diesel-powered ship, the first local BR drive-through ship and the first local vessel to carry a 'Dark Ages' name as then preferred by the British Railways Board. Although essentially a stern-loading train ferry, during the busy summer months she could also be used as a drive-through car ferry on the Dover-Boulogne route and her multi-purpose flexibility was seen as the model for all future tonnage.

Until 1970, BR car ferries had operated the Dover-Boulogne car ferry route while SNCF had operated from Calais to Dover in competition with Townsend Car Ferries. However, the year 1970 saw the most intensive efforts yet to concentrate all traffic towards the shortest route. Between mid-July and mid-September, some 64 weekly round sailings would be offered as opposed to just 38 in 1969. At the same time Boulogne sailings were cut from 78 to 66 during the same period. The reason for this dramatic change in policy lay at the door of the British Rail hovercraft division. Seaspeed had introduced twin SRN4 car ferry hovercraft onto the Dover-Boulogne route in 1968 and 1969 and during the next ten years, this unwanted competition was to rule the minds and planning of those who operated the service. The shipping division certainly suffered as a result of the hovercraft at a time when Townsend Car Ferries were heavily investing in new tonnage and also in their new route to Zeebrugge. British Rail, through their shipping and hovercraft subsidiaries competed with themselves. The 1970s were to see the gradual run down of the Dover-Boulogne car ferry services which were directed through Folkestone and British Rail/ SNCF going head to head with Townsend at Calais.

FOLKESTONE AND THE 'H' BOATS

The future of Folkestone as a cross-Channel port had been under threat for some considerable time and there were many

Above: The second *Maid of Orleans* was the first local steamer to enter service for the new British Railways in June 1949. She continued in service until the end of the 1975 season latterly operating rail-connected services between Dover and Calais. *(Don Smith/Phototransport.com)*

Left: The spare *Caesarea* was displaced from Weymouth and switched to the Short Sea Routes for the 1976 season. She is seen off service at berth 5 on Dover's Admiralty Pier. *(Ken Larwood)*

Below: The multi-purpose vessels *Hengist* and *Horsa* introduced vehicle ferry operations on the Folkestone services during the summer of 1972. Here is the *Horsa* alongside at berth 15 at Boulogne. *(Bruce Peter collection)*

The versatile **Vortigern** was the first BR diesel-driven ferry at Dover and Folkestone and initially operated trains from Dover to Dunkirk during the winter and passengers and cars to Boulogne in the summer. She soon became a regular fixture at Folkestone after which her appearances as a train ferry all but ceased. *(John Hendy collection)*

who believed that Dover could have easily accommodated the port's sailings. This was particularly so during the winter months when Folkestone played host to a single afternoon visit by the Calais-based steamer *Cote d'Azur.*

On the other hand there were those who failed to understand why British Rail paid dues to Dover Harbour Board when proper development at their own port of Folkestone would bring a multiplicity of benefits, not least no longer having to share facilities and infrastructure with competitors.

By 1970 most of the traditional railway ports had been converted to drive on-drive off with the addition of a linkspan – a bridge which would link ship to shore and across which cars would be driven directly into the ships.

During spring 1970, the British Railways Board made the historic announcement that at last Folkestone would become a vehicle ferry port and plans were unveiled for a £1 million upgrade and conversion of the port's facilities. At the same time £6.5 million would be awarded to construct two identical ferries with which to operate the new service. With no British yards being able to meet the requirements of the building contract, it was instead awarded to the Naval Dockyard at Brest. After years in the doldrums, Folkestone was at last given a new lease of life.

The two new ships, the *Hengist* and the *Horsa*, took up service in June and August 1972 although initially the former operated as a passenger-only vessel following damage and delays in the construction of the port's linkspan. Eventually, the new service commenced on 1st July and also included an overnight sailing to Ostend as BR had secured a 15 per cent share in the Belgian route. During much of the period under

review, the nationalised railway company's obsession with a Channel Tunnel and its effects saw them reluctant to build new ferries for the Short-Sea routes and both the *Hengist* and *Horsa* were earmarked for future service from Heysham to Belfast. Their after bridges were built expressly to allow astern navigation up the River Lagan into the Ulster port while it was also envisaged that their upper mezzanine decks would eventually be converted to cabins.

August and September 1972 proved to be groundbreaking months. With the *Horsa* in service on 8th August, the passenger steamer *Maid of Orleans* retired to Dover where in the worst gales of the summer, the 'Golden Arrow' steamer *Invicta* finally bowed out thereby allowing the 'Maid' to continue with the service the following day until closing it on 30th September. On the same day, the Calais steamer *Cote d'Azur* was withdrawn so that on 1st October it was no longer possible to cross the Dover Strait in a traditional passenger ferry.

The Dunkirk train ferry, the *Shepperton Ferry*, was also retired from service in late August leaving just the French flag *Twickenham Ferry* in service as the sole survivor of the route's original trio. She soldiered on until May 1974 when at the splendid age of 40 she was finally retired.

The 'Shepperton's' place in the fleet was taken by a converted ro-ro ship which was built for Stena Line in Norway. One of a trio of sister ships, the *Anderida* started service at Dover on the day after the 'Shepperton' was retired. With limited capacity and a passenger certificate for just 20, she was not a like for like replacement of the Tyne-built ship but filled a gap until her own withdrawal in July 1981. During this period she frequently served as a ro-ro vessel in the Irish Sea.

The **Earl Siward** was built as the **Dover** in 1965 by Swan Hunter for the Dover-Boulogne car ferry service. Changes in traffic trends saw her converted to drive-through operations and renamed in 1977 but operationally she was never a huge success. *(Ken Larwood)*

Sale listed in Dover's Wellington Dock during 1981 are the half-sisters **Anderida** and **Ulidia**. The former had entered service on the Dover-Dunkirk train ferry in 1972 while the latter had commenced operation at Stranraer two years later. They were both eventually sold to Greek owners. *(Jim Ashby)*

The *Dover's* half-sister *Holyhead Ferry I* appeared from the Irish Sea during early 1973 and again in 1974 when she was exchanged with the *Dover* which gave the Holyhead-Dun Laoghaire link much needed extra car carrying capacity. At the same time, the *Maid of Kent* was transferred to the seasonal Weymouth-Cherbourg route in 1974.

Meanwhile the *Maid of Orleans* continued in service operating seasonal train-connected services from Dover Western Docks (Marine Station) but was finally withdrawn from service in September 1975. Her place in the fleet was taken by the displaced Weymouth steamer *Caesarea* which again operated on a seasonal basis from both Dover and Folkestone until her own demise in October 1980. During the following year, the much travelled former Stranraer car ferry *Caledonian Princess* was also released from the Weymouth-Channel Islands route and served out the season becoming the very last steamship to operate in the Dover Strait.

CONVERSIONS

The reluctance of the nationalised railway company to build new tonnage for the Dover Strait in the shadow of Channel Tunnel construction, presented the local fleet with serious operational difficulties. Ever since the mid-1960s, the roll on-roll off (ro-ro) revolution demanded larger than ever vehicle decks and the ability to drive through the ships which carried the freight. Whereas stern-loading car ferries were fine for cars which could drive on board and swing around inside the ships in readiness for driving off the other end, this was totally impractical for large lorries. The only other alternative was to reverse the lorries on board but this was not only potentially dangerous but also time consuming. Ships don't make money when tied up in port and fast and efficient turn round periods are essential – particularly in Dover and Calais where there are inevitably other ships waiting to berth.

At this time, Townsend Thoresen were mopping up the freight traffic with a fleet of purpose-built drive-through ferries. Sadly the *Holyhead Ferry I*, the *Dover* and SNCF's *Chantilly*

(1966) were all built as stern-loading car ferries. The conversion of the French vessel to drive-through occurred during December 1975 to January 1976 and in New Year 1976 the *Holyhead Ferry I* was duly sent to the Tyne for similar work extending her commercial vehicle capacity from eight to 26. Delays at the yard during the £1.85 million conversion saw her miss the entire summer season as a result of which BR were forced to charter the spare Belgian Marine ship *Artevelde* between June and September. The errant ship finally returned as the *Earl Leofric* ready to take up the winter timetable. Her half-sister, the *Dover* was similarly converted to drive-through in Aalborg (Denmark) during the following spring and returned to service as the *Earl Siward* following her £1.96 million conversion.

These conversions were really only a stop-gap measure before new purpose-built tonnage could be ordered and the careers of the final BR steamers proved to be extremely short – just 16 years – before they were laid aside. Much had been promised on their behalf but developments in cross-Channel trade were overtaking them as soon as they were built and they proved to be inadequate for the blossoming ro-ro market.

A new Port Rapide was opened in the sand dunes at Dunkirk West during July 1976 reducing the crossing time to just 2 hours 15 minutes. Apart from the train ferry link it was hoped to interest freight operators in a new ro-ro service from Dover's Eastern Docks. The diminutive *Normannia* was first trialled but as she was a car ferry, her size prevented her from carrying more than a handful of lorries. The SNCF ferry *Compiegne* was tried at the end of November until the *Earl Leofric* was switched to the new link at the end of the year but the writing was on the wall and the service was quietly dropped from the schedules. What had once seemed like a good idea simply lacked the frequency that the freight operators demanded of their ferry services.

During 1978 and 1979, the elderly *Lord Warden* was sent to the Irish Sea for stints at Fishguard and Holyhead after which she was placed on the sale list. She was joined at her

Seen in the immediate pre-privatisation period, without her BR arrow funnel logos, the **St Christopher** was the second of a pair of Belfast-built ferries for the Dover-Calais service. They were both delivered late, the 'Christopher' not entering service at Dover until April 1981. These highly manoeuvrable twins suffered from inadequately dimensioned passenger accommodation and were later switched to Irish Sea routes. *(Bruce Peter collection)*

The **Horsa** is seen approaching the Admiralty Pier linkspan at Dover. *(Bruce Peter collection)*

The **St David** enjoyed a brief spell of service at Dover during spring 1983, relieving her half-sister **St Christopher** which had returned to Belfast for major modifications. *(FotoFlite)*

Newhaven lay-up by the *Normannia*, which had latterly been connected with the Channel Islands service from Weymouth. They had served their owners well but being steam powered they were expensive to operate and their inability to carry commercial vehicles meant that there was no longer a place for them within the fleet.

THE 'SAINTS' AND A FINAL THROW OF THE DICE

New Year's Day 1979 saw the creation of Sealink UK Ltd which replaced the British Rail Shipping & International Services Division.

The 1980s were to witness the creation of an entirely new generation of ferries capable of carrying freight on two decks and with double-width bow and stern doors to allow swift and easy disembarkation at both Dover and Calais. Sealink UK provided the Harland & Wolff built *St Anselm* and *St Christopher* while SNCF introduced the third named *Cote d'Azur* while competitors Townsend Thoresen replied with their three identical 'Spirit' class ferries. The scene was set for a period of intensive competition when at last the Sealink consortium were able to compete on something like a level playing field. The arrival of the *St Anselm* in October 1981 saw the retirement of the *Earl Leofric* while the *St Christopher*'s arrival in the following April saw the withdrawal of the *Earl Siward*. The slightly larger and more successful *Cote d'Azur* joined them during October replacing the *Compiegne*. The British twins were hampered by their lack of adequate passenger accommodation and as first envisaged, it was intended that they each should carry not many more than 600, it being believed that by 1980, hovercraft would be carrying the bulk of Channel passengers. However, the new ships entered service with passenger certificates for 1,000 which was soon increased by a further 200 when the after portion of their Bridge Decks were opened up and later by another 200 by extending their after accommodation. The twin ships were part of a four-ship building programme which represented the final major construction project for the nationalised railway company.

During spring 1982, SNCF ordered a second new ferry, their *Champs Elysees* with which it was hoped to revive the flagging fortunes of Boulogne. The ship duly entered service during October 1984 and from January 1985 she initially operated a single round sailing to Boulogne in addition to her scheduled Calais sailings. By March the Boulogne sailings were cut to just two a week and by July, the service was reduced to just one weekly Saturday crossing using the *St David* which had been introduced at Dover during March to run the Dover-Ostend service in replacement for the discontinued overnight sailings from Folkestone.

The de-nationalisation of Sealink UK Ltd occurred in July 1984 with its purchase by Sea Containers of Bermuda for £66 million.

NEWHAVEN

The Newhaven-Dieppe crossing was quite unlike any other cross-Channel service as it was a jointly owned operation. In 1862 the London Brighton & South Coast Railway had entered into a sharing agreement with the Chemins de Fer de l'Ouest. The exact British fraction was 37/56ths and was based on the length of the railway journey from Newhaven to the capital city while the French took the larger share. In practice this meant that the British owned about one-third of every ship and took the same amount of all the generated revenues whilst the French partners took the other two-thirds. Whilst this arrangement was acceptable to the Victorian railway companies, it was later to cause serious obstacles to the route's operation and future development.

POST-WAR REVIVAL

The Second World War had seen the losses of the British steamers *Paris* (1913) and *Brighton* (1933) while the French-crewed *Newhaven* and *Rouen* (1912) and the *Versailles* (1921) were not considered worth reconditioning at the war's end.

Prior to the start of hostilities, an order had been placed at Le Havre for replacements for the 1912 sisters. Originally to be named *Dieppe* and *Newhaven* their names were changed to *Londres* and *Vichy* before the former was seized on the stocks by the invading German army and eventually used as the coastal minelayer *Lothringen*. At the end of the war she was returned to Le Havre and, renamed *Londres*, entered service at Dieppe during April 1947. The sister ship was eventually named *Arromanches*, after the Normandy invasion beach, and entered service in summer 1947.

Meanwhile the railways in Britain were nationalised in 1948 and the sole survivor of the pre-war fleets was the 1928-built *Worthing*, the sister ship to the *Brighton* which had been lost at Dieppe in 1940. British Railways went back to Denny of Dumbarton for a replacement and the new *Brighton* (the sixth ship to carry that name) entered service in 1950. The vessel was a smaller but faster version of the Dover Strait steamer *Maid of Orleans* which Denny had built in the previous year. In the following year, SNCF returned to Le Havre builders Forges et Cie de la Méditerranée for the *Lisieux* of 1953. She was very much a smaller version of the *Cote d'Azur* which had been built by the same yard for the Calais-Folkestone crossing in August 1950. It can be seen that the new ships very much followed the trend of steamers on the route which required a shorter overall length in order to manoeuvre with ease within the confines of the River Ouse at Newhaven and the inner port at Dieppe.

The arrival on station of the *Lisieux* allowed British Railways to withdraw their pre-war steamer *Worthing* in May 1955 at which time SNCF transferred the ownership of the *Londres* which raised the Red Ensign and worked with a British crew ensuring that both partners supplied the Newhaven-Dieppe route with two ships.

In addition to the four passenger steamers, SNCF also

In readiness for privatisation in 1984, the **Hengist** appeared at Folkestone partly painted in a new livery which was eventually unveiled by the Harwich vessel **St Nicholas** during a visit to Dover in March. *(John Hendy)*

provided the three identical cargo vessels *Brest*, *Nantes* and *Rennes* in which increasing numbers of cars were crane loaded and shipped across the Channel while motorists travelled in the conventional steamer leaving port an hour later. Each of these motor vessels had a capacity for as many as 60 cars.

By 1960, the service had reached a stage in its development which demanded change. Annual passenger numbers using the route had declined by 29 per cent since 1955 whereas on the Short-Sea routes at Dover and Folkestone, they had risen by 34 per cent during the same period. Admittedly, some of this trend could be attributed to the fact that since 1956, the Dieppe-Newhaven crossing had become seasonal with the ships laid up between the end of October and the following Easter. However, the passenger steamers were (until March 1964) two-class vessels which required the duplication of all on-board facilities and added to this, their fast crossing times and fuel-thirsty engines meant that in a changing world they were never going to be economical ships to operate. The four steam ships were built to carry train-connected passengers to and from London and Paris via the most direct route between the capital cities. Yet at the same time when year on year, the number of motorists using the route was showing a marked increase, the percentage of foot passengers using boat trains was sharply dropping.

ENTER THE FALAISE

It was not surprising that the route's saviour was the long-awaited introduction of a car ferry. This was the versatile former Southern Railway Southampton steamer *Falaise* which had been built by Denny's in 1947 mainly for the seasonal St Malo route although she also saw work both on the Le Havre and Channel Islands links. It was stated at her launch that she was "intended primarily for the Channel Islands traffic but that she can also be used on the Dover, Folkestone and Newhaven services and short-sea cruises" and so the Southern had seen her very much as, what became known later, an 'inter-available' vessel. At the end of her first season, she had even briefly deputised on the Dover-Calais 'Golden Arrow' crossing for a period of one month, a schedule which was repeated in the following year.

British Railways had been seeking to close their loss-making Le Havre and St Malo routes for some years and after permission had finally been granted, the Le Havre steamer *Normannia* and the 17 year old *Falaise* were sent to the Tyne for conversion to car ferries. The *Falaise* left Southampton for Vickers Armstrong (Shipbuilders) Ltd in early January 1964. The two-class ship, with accommodation for 1,527 passengers and sleeping berths for 338, was totally gutted and transformed, re-emerging with a passenger certificate for 700 one-class passengers and a split-level garage capable of carrying 100 cars (75 on the Main Deck and 25 on the Mezzanine Deck above). If required, four lorries could be accommodated adjacent to her stern door which reduced the car numbers to just 80.

The first car ferry to test the new facilities at Newhaven and Dieppe was the Calais vessel *Compiegne* which was sent for trials early in 1964. Although she negotiated the River Ouse at Newhaven without problem, it was seen that berthing at Dieppe might cause her future difficulties.

After an inaugural excursion on Sunday 31st May 1964, the *Falaise* commenced commercial service at 10.00 on the following day reintroducing year-round schedules on the link.

The passenger steamer *Londres* had been withdrawn from service at the close of her 1963 season and soon passed to Greek owners while her French sister ship *Arromanches* followed suit in 1964. The newer *Lisieux* and *Brighton* continued to operate although their days were certainly numbered, particularly when in May 1964 SNCF ordered twin car ferries for the following season. The *Brighton* and *Lisieux* eventually closed the daily passenger service on 25th May 1965.

If British Railways and SNCF had ever had any doubts concerning the future of the Newhaven-Dieppe crossing, these were immediately extinguished by the unrivalled success of the new service. In 1963 fewer than 35,000 cars had used the route via the old lift on-lift off method. During the first year of the *Falaise*, the number rose to over 83,000 and in 1965 (the first year of the new French car ferries) to just over 175,000. During the same three years, the percentage of foot passengers

The **Falaise** was built as a passenger steamer for the Southampton services in 1947 but after the closure of the St Malo link in 1963 she was converted into a vehicle ferry, opening the Newhaven-Dieppe car ferry service in June 1964. She was later transferred to Weymouth where she ended her days operating to the Channel Islands. *(John Hendy)*

Above: A splendid view of the **Worthing** on passage from Newhaven to Dieppe, one of the three 25-knot services in operation during the 1950s. Built by Wm. Denny & Bros in 1928, the steamer was sold to Greek owners in 1955. Her sister ship **Brighton** (V) was lost at Dieppe in May 1940. *(FotoFlite)*

Bottom left: The Newhaven-Dieppe route was a joint service between BR and their French counterparts, SNCF. Here is the unsuccessful French-owned freight ship **Capitaine Le Goff** which operated the route between 1972 and 1978. Note the joint service flag on her stem. *(John Hendy)*

Below: The **Senlac** joined the Dieppe route in May 1973 having allowed the **Falaise** to transfer to Weymouth. She is seen during a period of industrial action early in 1982 when the slogan '**Save our Senlac**' was attached to her funnel. Sealink UK had previously notified their intention to withdraw from the Joint Service Agreement. *(Ken Larwood)*

arriving on boat trains dropped from almost 74 per cent to 42 per cent and continued to fall throughout the decade while overall passenger numbers continued to show a healthy increase.

TWIN FERRIES FOR SNCF

The first of the new £1.6 million SNCF ferries was launched at Nantes during November 1964 and named *Villandry* while her sister, *Valencay*, entered the water at St Nazaire in the following February.

Prior to their arrival, the service had experienced some difficulties with the *Falaise* hitting the pier at Dieppe in August 1964 and again at Newhaven during October. The *Normannia* from Dover was called in to deputise and thereafter became a regular visitor. During gales at Easter 1965, the *Falaise* managed to hit the East Pier at Newhaven causing considerable damage to her bow. Initially cars were once again crane loaded onto passenger ships before all vehicle traffic was re-routed via Dover. Two days later, the *Normannia* was hurriedly despatched westwards and took up service in place of the stricken car ferry.

The new *Villandry* arrived at Newhaven on her inaugural voyage during mid-May 1965, officially opening the new £330,000 terminal, but did not take up commercial crossings until the end of the month. The remaining two passenger steamers continued in service with the *Brighton* operating 'no passport' excursions at weekends allowing seven hours ashore for just 47/6d (£2.37). However, with the impending arrival of the *Valencay*, the *Lisieux* was withdrawn from service on 26th June and was chartered to the French Line (CGT) in the following month for a series of excursions running between St Malo and Jersey with a weekly connection to Torquay and later Weymouth. The service ended in September before the 12 year old ship was offered for sale, passing to Greek owners Agapitos in the following March for £240,000.

The *Valencay* duly commenced service on 7th July 1965 after which the smaller *Falaise* was switched to off-peak sailings.

Aesthetically, the new French twins bore certain similarities to the Calais-Dover car ferry *Compiegne* of 1958 and had continued the 45-degree drop in black hull paint below the foremast as introduced to SNCF by the Danish-built *Saint-Germain* in 1951. Following her conversion in 1964, the *Falaise* had spent her first season as a car ferry looking very bottom heavy with the line of the hull paint continuing aft in a straight line between her high fo'c'sle and stern. Happily, the introduction of her new French running partners saw this rather clumsy application modified and there is little doubt that the ship always looked far better in this guise.

The *Villandry* and *Valencay* were the first diesel-engined passenger ships on the route and also introduced other innovations which were to become commonplace. They were fitted with controllable-pitched propellers which gave them the required thrust by changing the angle of the blades which were in constant motion and were controlled from the bridge by the Master. Twin rudders helped give the ships far greater manoeuvrability and the fitting of bow-thrust units eased the ships' bows on and off their quays. Stern docking bridges were also fitted although these were little used and subsequently removed.

With capacity for as many as 1,200 passengers and 150 cars, the twin ferries were purely stern loaders and as they were built to replace three conventional cargo vessels, they also handled general cargo loaded by BR Brute design trolleys which

were towed on board by battery-electric tractors. Passenger luggage was also stored on the vehicle decks in tractor-driven luggage cages which saved the ships' public spaces from becoming clogged with baggage.

Looking to make savings in fuel, the crossing time was extended to 3 hours 45 minutes and each ship managed two round crossings each day which were no longer timed to especially coincide with convenient rail departure times from London or Paris.

In 1966, the *Brighton* was retained as spare vessel and again carried out a series of Wednesday and Sunday excursions before finishing on 18th September after which she was offered for sale. Meanwhile the cargo vessels *Nantes* and *Rennes* were sold to Metaxas of Greece although the third of the trio, the *Brest*, was retained and closed the traditional cargo service during mid-February. Thereafter she was used on both the Folkestone-Boulogne and Weymouth-Channel Islands runs before following her sisters to the same Greek owners in October 1967.

During late 1964, the British Railways fleet had adopted the new identity and livery of British Rail. Gone were the black hulls and distinctive buff, black-topped funnels to be replaced by monastral blue hulls and red funnels with the BR double-arrow logo. Although the Newhaven-Dieppe fleet changed hull colours, to show that this was a two-thirds French service, the three remaining vessels retained their buff funnel colours until in December 1967, the *Valencay* returned from overhaul sporting the historic joint-service flag thus clearly stating the route's independence and separate identity.

With traffic continuing to grow, during autumn 1970, the British Railways Board ordered a new ship from the Brest Naval Dockyard. Initially known simply as 'CF3', she followed the design of the new Folkestone-Boulogne ferries *Hengist* and *Horsa* which were then building at the same yard. The *Falaise* was now just too small and had been earmarked to open a new car ferry service linking Weymouth and Jersey in 1973.

CONTINUED RO-RO GROWTH

During the early 1970s, roll on-roll off traffic was growing at an unprecedented rate which prompted SNCF to acquire a specialist freight vessel in the form of the *Capitaine Le Goff*.

The vessel arrived at Dieppe in late July 1972 but berthing problems and manning arrangements prevented an early entry into service. Unfortunately the unpopular vessel proved both to be unstable and slow only managing a single round sailing each day. Following her final sailings in spring 1978 she was hastily sold to Saudi Arabian owners.

A visit at Newhaven by the new Folkestone car ferry *Hengist* en route to Dover from her builders at Brest on 7th June 1972, gave people in the Sussex town their first glimpse of the new breed of ferry and allayed local fears that the 'CF3' would not fit the port's linkspan.

A suitable name for the 'CF3' took some time to evolve. The British Railways Board were anxious to choose an English name associated with France and eventually the name *Senlac* was selected, after the site of the Battle of Hastings in 1066.

Meanwhile the *Falaise* sailed to Holyhead in January 1973 where she was prepared for the final stage of an illustrious career. Sadly boiler problems now began to plague the ship and after she had failed for a final time in August 1974, she was towed to Bilbao for scrapping. Without doubt, history will see this small steamer as the vessel that saved the Newhaven-Dieppe from closure and had later revitalised traffic to and from the Channel Islands.

The £4 million *Senlac* was officially named at a ceremony at Brest in March 1973 and duly arrived at Newhaven on 5th April. The ship boasted accommodation for 1,400 passengers and 210 cars (or 38 x 30ft lorries), double that of the vessel that she replaced. Although due in service with the 11.45 from Newhaven on 1st May, a strike saw her maiden departure put back by 24 hours. A further new passenger terminal was opened at the Sussex port that October.

The mid-1970s saw a tremendous expansion in roll on-roll off freight crossing the English Channel and the nationalised railway fleets of England, Belgium and France (by now all trading as Sealink) were inadequately prepared to deal with the traffic. Money was always tight and as the shadow of a future Channel Tunnel was always present, they were reluctant to invest in new tonnage at a time when many of the low-headroomed stern loaders already in service were comparatively new. The sensible and cheaper alternative was to convert existing tonnage to drive-through operation whilst stripping out vehicle decks and providing greater height for lorries. In the case of some vessels, this required major surgery involving the raising of the passenger decks above.

DRIVE-THROUGH

Following work on the Calais-based ferry *Chantilly* during the winter of 1975-76, and also two British steamships, the *Villandry* and *Valencay* were also earmarked for conversion. Approximately two-thirds of their after accommodation was raised by 56cm and with the extra headroom provided on their vehicle decks, they would be able to carry 20, rather than the previous ten, lorries. At the same time, the after docking bridges were removed while the adjacent observation lounges were extended in their place. The *Villandry* was first to depart to Le Havre during autumn 1976 followed a year later by her sister ship.

The *Villandry* returned to service in late March 1977 but French newspapers carried an alarming report suggesting that the route could be closed. BR admitted that it was certainly losing money but they were looking at ways of increasing traffic by evaluating the possibility of a new link to Le Havre.

New Year's Day 1979 saw the creation of Sealink UK Ltd, a wholly owned subsidiary of the British Railways Board and in 1981 it was announced that they intended to withdraw from the Newhaven-Dieppe Joint Service at the end of that year. In the meantime the British looked for cuts in the service, especially on night sailings, and felt that with a 50/50 share agreement they might at last start making profits with the *Senlac*. A record number of passengers were carried during 1981 but the route still managed to lose some £3.5 million.

Sadly during meetings in January 1982, Sealink UK Ltd and SNCF were unable to renegotiate the 1862 Joint Service Agreement and so the *Senlac* was to be sold. Strikes soon spread throughout the Sealink UK fleet but on 9th February, a breakthrough was finally made. The *Senlac* would be retained and partnered by the Calais-based *Chartres* while the *Villandry* would be sold and the *Valencay* downgraded to spare vessel. The French Government had promised SNCF financial backing to charter a larger Swedish ferry which would eventually replace the *Chartres*.

The arrival of the *Chartres* at Dieppe during May 1982 prompted an immediate dispute over manning levels and, until such time that matters were resolved, the *Senlac* sailed from Newhaven to Boulogne.

The redundant *Villandry* was busy on charter between Stranraer and Larne during the summer before being urgently called back to assist at Calais in August after a collision between the *Chantilly* and the new *Cote d'Azur*. She later became the stand-by vessel at Calais receiving the red SNCF funnel in December 1983 after Sealink UK Ltd had sold their one-third share in the vessel. Further charters took place between Holyhead and Dun Laoghaire and Heysham and Douglas (Isle of Man) before, in August 1984, the *Villandry* was eventually sold to Agapitos Brothers of Piraeus.

The need for a much larger ro-ro vessel was fulfilled by the charter of the spare Brittany Ferries vessel *Cornouailles* in January 1984. With capacity for 500 passengers and 205 cars

SNCF's **Valencay** was one of a pair of car ferries which joined the Dieppe-based fleet in 1965. She is seen going astern into the River Ouse at Newhaven before both she and her sister **Villandry** were converted to drive-through operations in 1977/78. *(Bruce Peter collection)*

SNCF's ***Chantilly*** was introduced on the Calais-Dover service in June 1966 but served her final years in the Dover Strait operating the train-connected services for which she received much unfavourable criticism. In 1986 she was transferred to the Dieppe station and is seen in the Dieppe Ferries livery before she was disposed of in the following year. *(Ken Larwood)*

or 40 trailers and 30 cars, her arrival on station saw the withdrawal of the *Valencay* even though she had been rostered to operate during that summer's peak season. However, strikes by the crews of the *Senlac* against the privatisation of Sealink UK Ltd saw the *Valencay* reactivated, running from Dieppe to Dover Western Docks at the end of May. However, by the end of the year she was on her way to a further career in Greek waters.

One of the first actions taken by the privatised Sealink British Ferries (now part of the Sea Containers Group) in October 1984 was to announce the British withdrawal from the Newhaven-Dieppe route as from the following March when the *Senlac* would be sold to SNCF. Chairman James Sherwood stated that as the *Senlac* was only able to make two round sailings each day (as opposed to the four of vessels based at Dover and Folkestone), this effectively meant that fares and retail and catering sales were half price. The French received subsidies from the State, regional and local levels whereas Sealink received no subsidies at all.

The *Senlac*'s finale under the Red Ensign proved to be the emotional last day of January 1985 after which the ship sailed to Le Havre for dry-docking. The summer of 1985 was the first peacetime summer since 1825 that a British vessel had not plied from the Sussex coast to Dieppe.

More French strikes greeted the *Senlac*'s return in full SNCF ownership during late February.

SOUTHAMPTON & WEYMOUTH

Perhaps of all the railway-owned and operated ports, Southampton was to see the greatest decline during the period of state ownership.

BACK ON TRACK - SOUTHAMPTON

The war had seen the loss of the passenger steam ships *Normannia* (1912), *Lorina* (1918) and *St Briac* (1924) and the cargo vessels *Fratton* (1925) and *Minster* (1924), the latter having been transferred to Southampton on the opening of the train ferry service from Dover to Dunkirk in October 1936. Sister ships *Whitstable* (in 1945) and *Hythe* (in 1949) were sent westwards from Dover to supplement the Southampton fleet while Denny's received orders for a new passenger ship and a cargo vessel. With the *Dinard* moving to Dover as a car ferry, the new passenger ship – which was originally destined for the Channel Islands service – was instead allocated to the St Malo link.

Following their liberation in May 1945, the *Isle of Guernsey* (1930) reopened the passenger service to Guernsey and Jersey before the Le Havre vessel *Hantonia* deputised and was eventually joined by the *Isle of Jersey* (1930) in October.

It fell to the *Autocarrier* to reopen the Jersey-France link in January 1946 although as St Malo was still under repair after severe war damage, Granville was instead substituted. By mid-April St Malo was back in business and the ship was also called upon to service Alderney before the *Brittany* (1933) returned from refit in June.

The cross-Channel route to Le Havre restarted in early 1947 using the *Autocarrier* and then the *Brittany* before in June the elderly *Hantonia* (1912) returned to service. With the new *Falaise* joining the fleet and opening up the service to St Malo on a twice-weekly basis in July, shipping services at Southampton finally returned to something like normal although the *Falaise* was forced to anchor in the roads and tendered to outside the French port until 1951 when the lock gates into the

The port of St Malo was badly damaged as a result of Allied bombing during the war and it was not until 1951 that the new *Falaise* (1947) was able to berth in the harbour rather than be tendered to in the Rance estuary. Astern of her is the *Brittany* of 1933 which operated the Channel Islands-France service until her sale in 1962. *(John Hendy collection)*

inner docks were finally reopened. At weekends the steamer was switched to the Channel Islands routes.

During the final month of the Southern Railway's existence, the new cargo vessel *Winchester* was delivered from Denny's.

BACK ON TRACK – WEYMOUTH

The shipping services from the Great Western Railway port of Weymouth, provided competition with the Southern Railway's services from Southampton.

The Great Western not only operated to the Channel Islands but also ran the St George's Channel route across the southern Irish Sea between Fishguard and Rosslare. At the end of the war, the company ordered twin passenger steam ships from Cammell Laird of Birkenhead to replace their war losses, one of which was destined to become the extra seasonal ship at Weymouth supplementing the services of the *St Helier* and *St Julien* (both 1925).

The cargo steamer *Sambur* (1925) reopened the Weymouth link in September 1945 and was followed in October by her sister ship *Roebuck* but it was not until mid-June 1946 that the passenger service was resumed with the *St Helier*. After spending her first summer on the Irish Sea, the first of the new post-war Birkenhead-built ships, *St David*, was transferred to Weymouth during September 1947 and operated for a month before returning to Fishguard – her only spell of service in the English Channel.

NATIONALISATION

On New Year's Day 1948, Southampton came under the control of British Railways (Southern Region) while Weymouth came under the wing of the new Western Region of British Railways. Fortunately this situation did not last long and at the start of November, the shipping services of the Dorset port were transferred to those of the Southern Region.

The *St Patrick*, the second of the post-war ships, arrived at Weymouth directly from her Birkenhead builders and entered service to the Channel Islands in February flying the Great

The *Ringwood* was one of the 1924-28 class of nine similar sister ships built for the Southern Railway's Dover/Folkestone and Southampton routes. Along with her sister ship, the *Haslemere*, she passed for scrap in 1959 when they were replaced by the *Elk* and *Moose*. *(John Hendy collection)*

Above: The *Caesarea* and *Sarnia* (pictured) were built at Cowes (Isle of Wight) for the Weymouth-Channel Islands route in 1960/61 by which time the rival route from Southampton was being run down before closing in May 1961. In order to placate the former Southern port, they were given Southern names rather than those of the former Great Western Railway. *(Bruce Peter collection)*

Left: The cargo ship *Winchester* is seen alongside at Weymouth after she was switched there from Southampton in 1965. Dating from 1949, the vessel was unable to carry unit loads and was sold for use as a Greek cruise ship in 1971. *(Ken Larwood)*

Below: The *Caesarea* alongside at Weymouth Quay. The new ships provided unprecedented comfort and luxury when compared with their pre-war predecessors. *(Ken Larwood)*

The cargo vessels **Elk** and **Moose** joined the Southampton fleet in 1959 replacing the pre-war coal burners. The **Elk** made the final railway sailing from Southampton in September 1972 after which the cargo services were switched to Portsmouth. Both ships were sold to Greek operators. *(FotoFlite)*

Western Railway house flag and in the company's full livery. She retired to the Irish Sea during the winter months but was to return to the Channel Islands services for every summer until being moved to the Dover Strait late in 1964. During this period she retained her Great Western red, black-topped funnel as her owners were the Fishguard & Rosslare Railways & Harbours Company, a subsidiary of the British Transport Commission.

With the slow return to normality came the reintroduction of excursions with the *Falaise* taking up the reins of the lost *St Briac* making long weekend cruises both to the Channel Islands and also to the French coastal ports either end of the high season. The third summer ship at Weymouth also allowed day trips to be operated to Guernsey.

During the early 50s, three ships of note entered the cross-Channel fleet on the Western Channel. We have already seen that the Folkestone steamer *Isle of Thanet* made supplementary summer Friday night crossings from Southampton to Guernsey in 1949 and from 1952 until 1958. In 1950 the Harwich steamer *Duke of York* was transferred to Southampton to operate a twice-weekly sailing to Cherbourg, also being utilised to operate

a weekend sailing to Guernsey. The Cherbourg route had unsuccessfully been tried between the wars and the attempt to revive it was not repeated in 1951. However, with the lock gates repaired at St Malo in time for the 1951 summer season, it was anticipated that passenger numbers would swell significantly and so the Holyhead steamer *Princess Maud* was introduced to operate a twice-weekly service in addition to the Friday night sailing to Guernsey. The car ferry *Dinard* was brought back from Dover during summer 1952 to operate a weekend sailing on her old route to St Malo but, with limited accommodation and a lack of cabins, was unsuccessful.

A new *Normannia* commenced service from Southampton to Le Havre in March 1952 and allowed the 40 year old veteran *Hantonia* to pass for scrap.

Throughout the 50s, the Channel Islands became an increasingly popular holiday destination and at peak periods the pre-war ships were hard pressed to cope. There were inevitable complaints concerning outdated facilities and over crowding and meetings were held between island officials and representatives of the British Transport Commission to try and resolve the problems. In 1955, it was agreed to deepen the harbour at St Helier (Jersey) while long overdue replacements would be ordered for the 30 year old *St Helier* and *St Julien*.

SOUTHAMPTON – DECLINE AND FALL

Although passenger numbers to the Channel Islands were continuing to rise, the shipping services were suffering as a result of increased competition from the air. The Southampton-Le Havre and St Malo services were also in decline and in late 1958, only one ship was required to operate a reduced service while the *Brittany* was also laid up for the winter.

The old cargo steamers *Whitstable*, *Haslemere* and *Ringwood* (all with limited passenger accommodation) were replaced by the modern motor vessels *Elk* and *Moose* during late 1959 at which time the passenger steamer *Isle of Jersey* was also withdrawn from service. At Weymouth the *St Patrick* was retained during the winter period and was officially

The **St Helier** (pictured) and her sister **St Julien** were delivered to the Great Western Railway in 1925 and reliably maintained the Weymouth-Channel Islands link until replaced in service by the **Caesarea** and **Sarnia**. *(John Hendy collection)*

Above: The ***Maid of Kent*** was switched to the seasonal Weymouth-Cherbourg link in 1974 where she became a great favourite. She remained in service until the end of the 1981 season by which time she had become the very last railway-operated cross-Channel steamship. *(Ken Larwood)*

Left: The ***Winchester*** is seen at Weymouth in her new British Rail livery. During 1966, shortly before its closure, she deputised on the Folkestone-Boulogne cargo service. *(Ken Larwood)*

Below: The failure of the ***Falaise*** during the peak season of 1974 saw BR hastily arrange a charter of the Swedish ferry ***Svea Drott***. The vessel proved to be so successful that she was purchased in December 1974, eventually becoming Weymouth's ***Earl Godwin***. Built according to comparatively lax Swedish safety regulations, it proved unexpectedly costly and complex to bring her into line with British standards. *(Bruce Peter collection)*

transferred to BR ownership in December after which she gained a BR buff funnel. Meanwhile the winter timetable from Southampton showed just one round sailing each week to the Channel Islands but the Hampshire port's loss was certainly Weymouth's gain.

In June 1960 came the announcement that the two larger, one-class, ships, then under construction by J Samuel White at East Cowes (Isle of Wight), would operate on the shortest sea route (i.e. Weymouth) and that the Southampton service would close, making annual savings of £209,000. At the end of the season, the *St Helier*, *St Julien* and *Isle of Sark* were all withdrawn and during early December the new *Caesarea* made her debut. After 119 years, in May 1961 the Southampton service was terminated by the *Isle of Guernsey*, after which she was briefly switched to Weymouth until the arrival of the *Sarnia* in the following month.

The *Brittany* was also withdrawn in 1962 after which time the *St Patrick* operated a reduced service between Jersey and St Malo.

With the formation of the British Railways Board in January 1963 came news that a survey had indicated that there was no public demand for a car ferry on the Le Havre route. Nevertheless, Norwegian entrepreneur Otto Thoresen proved otherwise with his revolutionary bright orange drive-through 'Viking' ferries which took the Western Channel by storm when introduced on the Cherbourg and Le Havre routes in the summer of 1964.

By this time the end was in sight for the traditional railway operated Le Havre and St Malo services whose closure would conveniently make available two ships which could be converted to car ferries for Dover and Newhaven. The *Normannia*'s place on the Le Havre route was briefly taken by the *St Patrick* in December 1963 until such time that she closed the route in the following May. She then opened the seasonal St Malo service which finished during late September when cross-Channel railway passenger services from Southampton finally ceased. The *St Patrick* then moved to lay-up at Newhaven where she was repainted in the new British Rail livery in preparation for her further career in the Dover Strait.

In May 1964 the Marine Workshops at Southampton were also closed and that December the old cargo ship *Sambur* was retired followed by her sister *Roebuck* in the following February. They were replaced in March 1965 by the *Winchester* from Southampton. However, the traditional methods of cargo handling were changing and in June 1969 BR and Commodore Shipping signed an agreement to share container loading facilities in the islands. The *Winchester* was not suitable for this traffic and was withdrawn from service in late December 1970, being replaced by the Associated Humber Line's *Selby*. Although it was originally stated that the new container link would be operated from Southampton, a change of plan saw Portsmouth become the UK cargo terminal and a year later Fisher's *Jersey Fisher* and *Guernsey Fisher* were both taken on a five-year charter. The new service commenced in January 1972 with the *Elk* and *Moose* being retained for the Guernsey tomato traffic. The *Elk* made the last ever railway ship sailing from Southampton at the end of September 1972 and in the following month both she, the *Moose* and the *Selby* were withdrawn from service.

CAR FERRIES

During April 1972, BR made the historic announcement that a drive-on car ferry service would be introduced for the 1973 season. Made redundant at Newhaven by the arrival of the *Senlac*, the *Falaise* was sent to Holyhead for modifications and made her maiden commercial crossing on the first day of June 1973. Jersey was able to immediately accept the traffic but the authorities at Guernsey had failed to build a linkspan and so cars were lifted on and off during the first season.

The service was an immediate success and very soon there were calls for roll on freight to be carried. Unfortunately, in this respect the *Falaise* was found wanting and serious boiler troubles saw her fail at Weymouth during August 1974. BR were fortunate that they were able to charter the Swedish car ferry *Svea Drott* (1966) at short notice until in late September the *Caledonian Princess* was brought in to take her place. The *Normannia* from Dover later arrived and during December the *Svea Drott* was purchased and sent to Holyhead for lengthy modifications before she emerged as the *Earl Godwin* ready to take up the service in February 1976.

There was a great demand for a multi-purpose service (i.e. cars, freight and passengers) and this was implemented for the 1976 season using the *Earl Godwin* and the *Caledonian Princess*. Of the two passenger steamers, the *Sarnia* was retained for the peak season whilst the *Caesarea* was switched to the Dover station making her last scheduled sailing to the islands in October 1975.

The multi-purpose service commenced in May 1976 and its immediate popularity saw the purchase of Townsend Thoresen's *Viking II* (1964) in December that year. She was sent to Holyhead to be made ready for her new role and as the *Earl William* commenced service from Portsmouth late in January 1978 replacing both the container service and the Channel Islands' final passenger steamer *Sarnia* which finished in July 1977. The Portsmouth service had been commenced by the *Earl Godwin* in the previous November and with the new link quickly becoming a great success, the whole of the BR Channel Islands service had been completely renewed and reorganised within the period of five years. Such was its popularity that the 1978 summer saw an unprecedented three sailings a day to the islands.

The *Caledonian Princess* was replaced in the fleet by the *Earl Granville* (ex *Viking 4*) which was both rebuilt and re-engined before she took up the sailings from Portsmouth in March 1981 allowing the 20 year old steamer to move to Dover where she replaced the *Caesarea*.

The year 1981 also saw the end of the turbine steamer *Maid of Kent* (1959). Replaced at Dover in 1974 by the *Holyhead Ferry I*, a new niche had been found for her at Weymouth from where she operated a new seasonal service to Cherbourg during April. The ship became immensely popular and was given a rousing send off when on 2nd October 1981 she sailed to Cherbourg on her final sailing. However, no sooner had she completed this when the *Earl William* failed and so the *Maid of Kent* was retained to operate weekend sailings to Guernsey until the end of the month. She became the final railway-owned cross-Channel steam ship in operation.

For the 1982 season, the *Ailsa Princess* (1971) was transferred from the Stranraer-Larne link and restarted the crossing in April.

In July 1984, Sea Containers took over the ships and ports of Sealink UK Ltd and the railway era came to an end. Within two years, the excellent service which had been created by Sealink UK Ltd was in tatters.

Above: The *Canterbury* spent most of her post-war career operating on the seasonal Folkestone-Boulogne and Calais services, regularly deputising on the 'Golden Arrow' route during the winter periods when the *Invicta* was undergoing overhaul. *(Michael Woodland)*

Left top: The *Isle of Thanet* is seen awaiting sale in Dover's Wellington Dock during 1964. The design of her graceful stern represented a change from the counter to the cruiser style and allowed for fast stern-first approaches to her berths. *(John Hendy)*

Below: The Southampton-St Malo steamer *Dinard* was built in 1924 but was converted to a lift on-lift off car ferry for the Dover-Boulogne service in 1946. Entering service in the following June, in 1952 she was fitted with stern-loading arrangements and was not withdrawn until 1958 in anticipation of the arrival of the new *Maid of Kent*. *(FotoFlite)*

The **Hampton Ferry** and her twin sisters were built on the Tyne in 1934/35 but did not enter service on the Dover-Dunkirk train ferry service until Dover's train ferry dock was ready for use in October 1936. Notice the white positioning spike on her stern on which her linkspans would be positioned, thereby ensuring the correct alignment of the rails both ashore and afloat. *(Jim Ashby collection)*

A wonderfully reflective view of the **Hampton Ferry** at rest in Dover's Wellington Dock. The ship was the first of the trio to be withdrawn and was replaced in service by the **Vortigern** in 1969. *(Michael Woodland)*

Dover's first purpose-built car ferry was the ***Autocarrier*** of 1931. Originally proposed as the tenth of a series of fast cargo vessels, she was converted on the stocks and took up the Dover-Calais service in opposition to Townsend's ***Forde*** in May 1931. During the post-war period she served mainly from Folkestone until her withdrawal in 1954. *(FotoFlite)*

The ***Hampton Ferry*** at sea. She could always be recognised from her sisters as the drop in hull paint was at a much shallower angle. *(FotoFlite)*

Lord Warden

The first purpose-built, stern-loading car ferry in the English Channel was the third-named *Lord Warden* of 1952. A product of the Denny yard in Dumbarton, her 120 cars were initially crane loaded at Dover until the Eastern Docks Car Ferry Terminal was opened in June 1953. The vessel very soon proved to be a victim of her own success and ended her career in the Irish Sea serving on the Holyhead-Dun Laoghaire route in 1979.

The *Lord Warden*'s stern gates came in for much criticism following the loss of Stranraer's *Princess Victoria* in January 1953 as Denny's had designed similar doors for both ships. Towards the end of her career, the 'Warden's' doors were raised and strengthened. As can be seen in the image of her alongside Newhaven's *Senlac* in Dover's Wellington Dock during January 1978, the basic design of car ferries had greatly developed in the 21 years between each first entering service.

(Photos credits: Page 60 top Jim Ashby, bottom Ken Larwood; Page 61 top FotoFlite, middle Bruce Peter collection, bottom John Hendy)

Following the withdrawal of the *Canterbury* in 1964, British Rail switched the former Great Western Railway steamer *St Patrick* from Weymouth to the Dover Strait where she was principally engaged on the summer Folkestone-Boulogne link until sold to Greek owners in 1971. *(Ken Larwood)*

A powerful view of the flagship *Invicta* arriving at Calais with her 'Golden Arrow' passengers destined for Paris Gare du Nord. It is today unthinkable that such a vessel could ever be employed to operate a single round sailing each day. *(Bruce Peter collection)*

Above: The ***Shepperton Ferry*** going astern towards Dover's train ferry dock on her arrival from Dunkirk. The raised black balls on her main mast indicate that she is using her bow rudder. *(Ken Larwood)*

Left: The 'Shepperton's' replacement was the small ***Anderida*** which BR purchased on the stocks in Norway from the Swedish company Stena Line. The motor vessel later spent much of her time in the Irish Sea before being laid aside in 1981. *(FotoFlite)*

Below: A fine view of the Dover Strait's final traditional passenger steamer coming astern into Folkestone after a lively crossing from Calais during her 1976-80 stint on the Short Sea Routes. The ***Caesarea*** stern lifts as she approaches berth 1 allowing her screws to clear the water. *(Don Smith/Phototransport.com)*

Top left: Passengers gaze outboard from the **Maid of Kent**'s spacious teak-planked Boat Deck – a classic scene on a railway steamer. The funnel of the **Caledonian Princess** can be seen beneath the lifeboats. *(Bruce Peter collection)*

Top right: Inboard, the **Maid of Kent** represented a new design approach for railway shipping as British Railways' recently established Design Panel selected Ward & Austin, led by Neville Ward, to devise the interiors, which made extensive use of wipe-clean Formica and vulcanised rubber. Here we see the vessel's lounge-bar. *(Bruce Peter collection)*

Middle right: The **Maid of Kent**'s Tea Bar with circles on the floor and matching ceiling recesses to break the monotony of a wide, low-ceilinged space. (Bruce Peter collection)*r*

Right: The restaurant on the **Caesarea** was the work of BR's in house design team and was far more traditional than that in her sister **Sarnia**. *(Bruce Peter collection)*

Left: Another deck scene on board the *Maid of Kent*. *(Bruce Peter collection)*

Below: The *Maid of Kent* was informally known as the 'pocket liner' when she entered service from Dover to Boulogne in May 1959. She was the last local railway steamer to be built by Denny of Dumbarton but was later hampered by being a pure car ferry without sufficient vehicle deck headroom to cater for the increasing volumes of freight lorries on offer from the mid-1960s. *(Michael Woodland)*

Bottom: The *Maid of Kent* captured later in her career with arrows on her funnel. *(FotoFlite)*

Above: The *Dover* entered service from Dover to Boulogne in June 1965 and, as well as being the final steamship built for service at the port was also the first local ship to be delivered in the new livery of British Rail. She is seen in April 1966 leaving for her first overhaul on the Tyne. *(John Hendy)*

Left: The *Dover*'s plush forward saloon had concealed lighting and wall-to-wall curtaining. The design of the vessel's passenger accommodation was another success for Ward & Austin. *(Bruce Peter collection)*

Bottom left: The cafeteria on the *Dover* with robust fixed seating and tables. *(Bruce Peter collection)*

Below: A seating saloon on the *Dover*. Such spaces were considered a major enhancement over older tonnage as they guaranteed all passengers a seat indoors – very welcome in inclement weather. *(Bruce Peter collection)*

Left: Clouds of black smoke issue from the *Earl Siward's* funnel as the vessel raises steam in preparation for her departure. Turbine vessels used a great deal more fuel than motor ships as their boilers required to be kept at working pressure whether at sea or during loading operations in port. *(Kenny Whyte)*

Below: The *Dover's* conversion to drive-through operations took place at Aalborg (Denmark) during the winter of 1976/77. She reappeared as the *Earl Siward* with no fewer than 12 lifeboats but her reign was short and in 1981 she was sold on for service in Cyprus before returning to the UK as a floating nightclub in the north-east. *(Bruce Peter collection)*

Bottom: The *Dover's* half-sister was the *Holyhead Ferry I* which after 1973 began to spend more time in the Dover Strait during which time the *Dover's* extra car capacity was required on the Irish Sea. Converted to drive through on the Tyne during the winter of 1975/76, she reappeared very late as the *Earl Leofric* and was soon laid aside and sold for scrap in 1981. Due to her delayed return from conversion, BR were forced to charter to the spare Belgian car ferry *Artevelde*. *(Ken Larwood)*

Above: The *Vortigern*'s main vehicle deck showing her railway lines and also the hanging Mezzanine Decks which allowed extra cars to be carried during the main tourist season. *(Jim Ashby collection)*

Below: The much travelled ***Caledonian Princess*** was switched to the Dover Strait to work the train-connected services during 1981 after which she was sold for nightclub use on the Tyne. During her final season she worked mainly from Dover to Calais and Boulogne but is unusually seen leaving Folkestone. *(Ken Larwood)*

Below: Bow-in on an afternoon visit to Calais, the ***Horsa*** will have discharged her rail-connected passengers at the adjacent Gare Maritime while vehicle traffic runs ashore in the traditional manner. *(Jim Ashby collection)*

Top: Sister ship *Hengist* is seen turning off Dover's Eastern Docks. During their early years both the 'H' Boats, as they were informally known, were regular visitors to the port but later became exclusively Folkestone-based vessels. *(Bruce Peter collection)*

Above left: The *St Christopher* comes astern from Calais into Dover's Eastern Docks. *(Ken Larwood)*

Above right: The *St David* leaves the Admiralty Pier ready to cross the harbour to take up service to Calais. *(Jim Ashby collection)*

Left: With BR arrows removed from her funnels prior to privatisation, the *St Anselm* arrives at Dover's Admiralty Pier berth to unload train-connected passengers following the ending of Folkestone's association with this traffic in June 1984. *(Jim Ashby collection)*

Left: The sixth named **Brighton** served on the Newhaven-Dieppe route between 1951 and 1966 and was the route's final traditional passenger steamer. Her lines very much followed those of the earlier **Maid of Orleans** which was also a product of the Denny, Dumbarton yard in 1949. *(Bruce Peter collection)*

Above: The Brest-built **Senlac** followed Folkestone's **Hengist** and **Horsa** into service in May 1973. Heavy losses on the route eventually saw the vessel transferred to French ownership in 1985 before her sale to Greece two years later. *(Bruce Peter collection)*

Left: British Rail's ferries often contained modern artworks by well-known British artists and sculptors. The **Senlac**'s forward stairwell had a bas relief by Franta Belsky mural which depicted 'Dark Age' images similar to those found in the earlier near-sisters **Hengist** and **Horsa**. *(Bruce Peter collection)*

Below: The **Senlac**'s cafeteria had brass panels based on parts of the Bayeux Tapestry. *(Bruce Peter collection)*

Below: One of the **Senlac**'s lounge spaces. *(Bruce Peter collection)*

Newhaven in its prime with the **Senlac** alongside, the harbour tug **Meeching** assisting with the port's dredging while the classic Blue Star cargo vessel **Gladstone Star** discharges at the East Quay. The **Meeching** was built at Appledore (Devon) in 1960 and remained in service at the port following privatisation until sold for further trading in 1999. *(John Hendy)*

The Southern Railway's Southampton 'Isles' were the mainstay of the Channel Islands route from their introduction in 1930 until all passenger traffic was directed through Weymouth in May 1961. Here the **Isle of Jersey** enters the Western Solent and passes the Needles on her way into Southampton. It is of interest that passengers were permitted to use the fo'c'sle. *(FotoFlite)*

The third of the Southampton 'Isles' class vessel was the modified *Isle of Sark* of 1932. While her unusual maierform bow is obvious, she was the first railway ship to be fitted with Denny-Brown fin stabilisers and thus earns her claim to fame. With the demise of the Southampton services, she was sold for scrapping in 1960. *(FotoFlite)*

Seen alongside at Weymouth Quay, the former Great Western Railway cargo ship *Roebuck* (pictured) and her sister *Sambur* faithfully served the Channel Islands between 1925 until their withdrawal in 1964 and 1965. *(Ken Larwood)*

Top: During her first year based at Weymouth (1973), the ***Falaise*** was only able to use a linkspan to discharge cars at Jersey as the authorities at Guernsey failed to provide a loading bridge until 1974. Here she is loading at St Helier during her initial season when she at last appeared in service with a BR red funnel. (*Jim Ashby collection*)

Above left: The ***Caesarea*** is seen arriving at St Peter Port (Guernsey) during the late 60s. (*Bruce Peter collection*)

Left: Towards the end of her career, the diminutive ***Normannia*** began to spend a greater amount of time serving the Channel Islands but here she is high and dry in the Inner Harbour at Dover following a holing incident in July 1974. (*AG Jones/John Hendy collection*)

73

Cash desk

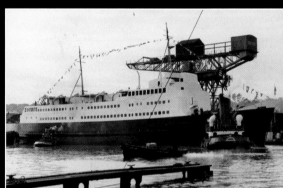

Above: A corner of the *Caesarea*'s restaurant, showing a table setting and, to the rear, the 'caged' hatch where the waiters would hand money to the cashier and collect a receipt. The white linen and polished cutlery suggests a genteel dining experience whereas the bulkhead detailing infers that there was a need for a remarkable degree of security! *(Bruce Peter collection)*

Top right: A general view of the *Caesarea*'s dining saloon. The vessel's interior was by the BTC's 'in house' architects. *(Bruce Peter collection)*

Middle right: The *Caesarea* is seen in the River Medina following her launch at Cowes in January 1960. The black hull paint of both sisters was later raised. *(Bruce Peter collection)*

Right: The *Sarnia* alongside at Weymouth Quay quietly awaits the arrival of her boat trains from London Waterloo. *(Ken Larwood)*

Top: The **Sarnia** at Weymouth. *(Ken Larwood)*

Above left: Part of a reclining seat lounge on the **Caesarea**. (*Bruce Peter collection*)

Above right: The **Caesarea** departing from Dover for Boulogne in August 1979. During her 1976-80 period of service in the Dover Strait, she operated between Easter and the end of September running two sailings a day involving, Dover, Folkestone, Calais and Boulogne. *(John Hendy)*

Left: Although outwardly sister ships, the interior of the **Caesarea** was the work of the head of British Railways' 'in house' Architects' Department, Dr Curtis, whose demands for extensive changes to the vessel's structure incurred the wrath of the naval architects. Ward & Austin's design for the **Sarnia** was, however, far more modern than the rather heavy and utilitarian interior of the **Caesarea** and Curtis was never asked to work on another railway ship! *(Bruce Peter collection)*

Above: Before moving eastwards to the Dover Strait in December 1964, the **St Patrick** served a period working from Southampton's Outer Dock. With both the Le Havre vessel **Normannia** and the St Malo vessel **Falaise** away undergoing conversion to car ferries, it was left to the 'Paddy' to officially close both routes. She became the first Southern Region ship to be painted in the new livery. *(Don Smith/Phototransport.com)*

Below: Here is the **St Patrick** coming astern into Folkestone Harbour following her move to the Dover Strait where she served between 1964 and 1971. *(Ken Larwood)*

Below: The former AHL vessel **Selby** is seen alongside at Weymouth. Built in 1959, the cargo ship was converted to a container ship at Holyhead in 1973 for use on the Heysham-Belfast service. She eventually replaced the **Winchester** on the Channel Islands link but after the introduction of the 'Fisher' twins was switched to Weymouth to cater for the Guernsey tomato trade. She was sold out of service early in 1973. *(Ken Larwood)*

Top: The *Maid of Kent* in her new Weymouth home following her transfer from Dover in 1974. The vessel remained registered in her former port but became a firm favourite on the seasonal Cherbourg link until replaced by the *Ailsa Princess* (later *Earl Harold*). *(John Hendy collection)*

Left: The *Svea Drott* was hastily brought in following the failure of the *Falaise* in August 1974. She was later purchased and became the *Earl Godwin*. *(Bruce Peter collection)*

Below: The containerised cargo vessel *Jersey Fisher* and her sister *Guernsey Fisher* were chartered for the Channel Islands services in 1972, initially operating from Southampton but later being transferred to Portsmouth. In 1977 the new ro-ro service made them both redundant and their charters were terminated. *(Jim Ashby collection)*

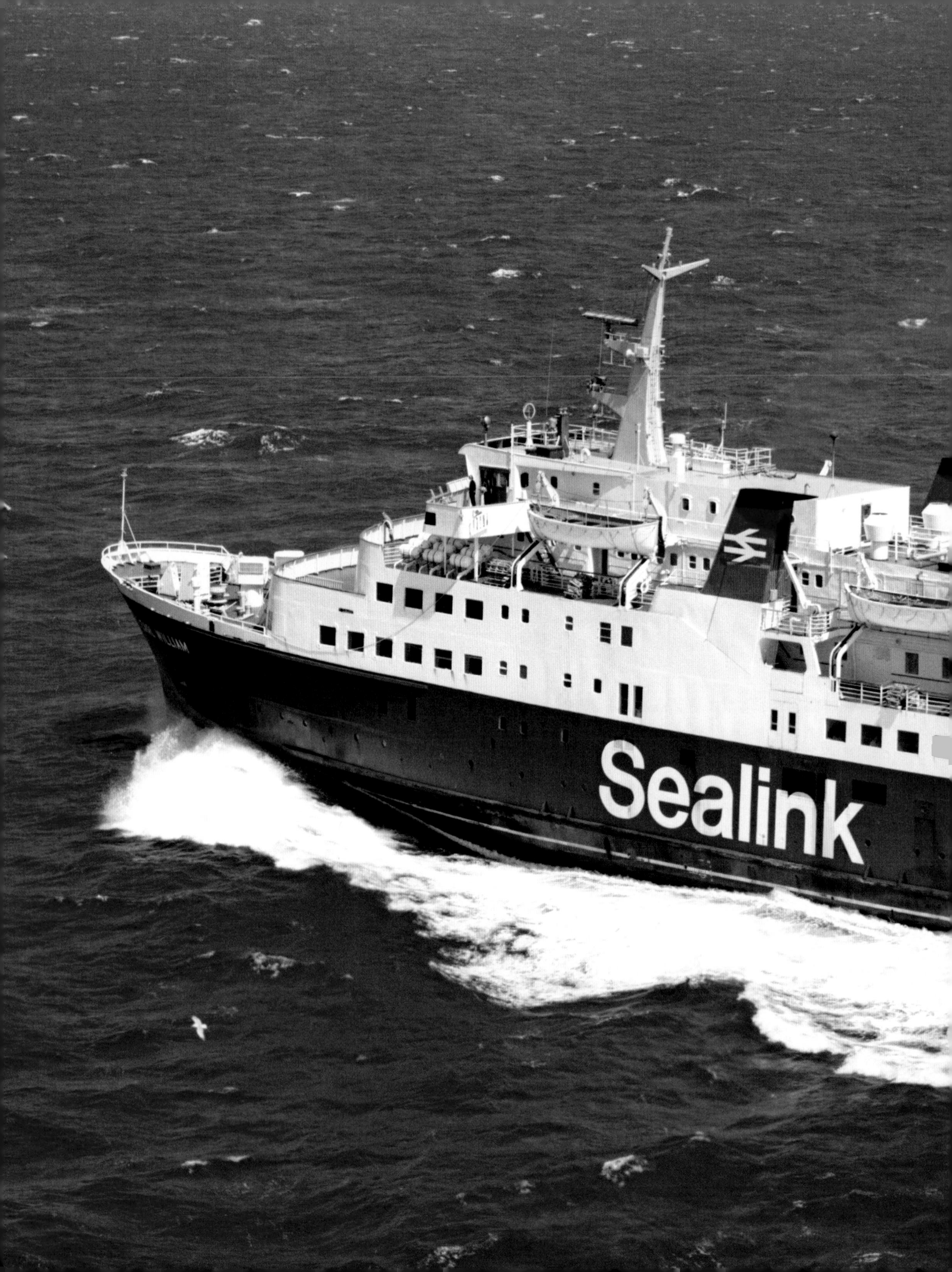
Sealink

Built in Norway in 1964, the *Earl William* was originally Thoresen Car Ferries' *Viking II* and operated on the routes between Southampton and Cherbourg/ Le Havre following on from British Rail's withdrawal from the port in 1963. The new operation was an immediate success and called into question BR's decision to end all passenger services from the Hampshire port. Acquired by BR in 1976 and converted for Channel Islands use at Holyhead, from January 1978 the renamed *Earl William* was a great success on the new Portsmouth link and allowed Weymouth to rid itself of the final passenger steamer *Sarnia*. (FotoFlite)

EARL WILLIAM

LONDON

The peripatetic *Caledonian Princess* served the Channel Islands between 1974 and 1981 after which she was switched to Dover. In order to make her more suitable for the carriage of large numbers of foot passengers, a modification at Immingham in 1976 added the large after deckhouse and filled in most of her after outside promenades. *(Bruce Peter collection)*

The *Earl Godwin* is seen having moved off her Weymouth berth in order to go astern out of the harbour. She remained in Channel Islands service until 1990 when she was sold to Italian buyers. *(Bruce Peter collection)*

A good view of the facilities at Weymouth adjacent to the town's busy pleasure beach. The former Stranraer vessel **Ailsa Princess** is alongside and ready to sail for Cherbourg. *(Jim Ashby collection)*

In January 1978 the company opened a Channel Islands service from Portsmouth which had far better road connections than Weymouth and was therefore better suited to the carriage of freight. The larger Viking Line vessel **Viking 4** (of 1973) was later purchased and converted to become the **Earl Granville**, taking over the Portsmouth service from the **Earl William** in March 1981. The 'William' was then switched to Weymouth in place of the **Caledonian Princess**. *(Ferry Publications Library)*

Sealink's Continental Partners

D ue to the nature of their through railway services to a host of European destinations, British Railways enjoyed a close and fruitful partnership with their French, Belgian and Dutch partners. When in November 1969 it was agreed that the Continental fleets should also adopt the trading name 'Sealink', this appeared to be the natural outcome of this co-operation.

The Sealink legend was first applied to the British ships on the introduction of the *Hengist* and *Horsa* in 1972 and upon the rest of the fleet in the following year. The railways of France had been nationalised in 1938 and apart from the historic joint Newhaven-Dieppe service, the Dover-Calais/ Dunkirk services were also closely linked. When British Railways became British Rail in 1965, the livery change was also reflected with the adoption of blue hulls and red funnels to which later the letters 'SNCF' were added in white. During the 60s, the joint BR/ SNCF services had traded as 'The Big Fleet' and from 1980 as 'the Flagship Service' on the Calais route.

ALA - ANGLETERRE-LORRAINE-ALSACE SA DE NAVIGATION

The two French-flagged ships which were not owned by SNCF were the train ferries *Twickenham Ferry* and her successor *Saint Eloi*.

The Angleterre-Lorraine-Alsace SA de Navigation was born in February 1927 when the London Midland & Scottish Railway (LMS) formed a French subsidiary in co-operation with Rothschild's Bank (via their subsidiary company SAGA) to operate an overnight route between Tilbury and Dunkirk. Four elderly vessels were duly transferred from the Irish Sea and the service commenced in May 1927. The link proved to be a financial failure but was taken over by the Southern Railway who switched the service to Folkestone as from May 1932. In the following year SAGA withdrew from the operation leaving the Southern in complete control. Once more, traffic was light but on the commencement of the Dover-Dunkirk train ferry service on 4th October 1936, the Folkestone link had ceased on the previous night. In readiness for the new service, the *Twickenham Ferry* was sold to ALA for £150,000 and hoisted the French flag, her port of registry becoming 'Dunkerque' rather than London.

Right through the BR era the ship continued to operate in the black hull and buff, black-topped funnels but after British Rail had been created in 1965, the *Twickenham Ferry* was at last given her own unique identity, appearing with red funnels and the ALA monogram in a white oval. The vessel outlived her sister ships but was finally withdrawn in May 1974 in preparation for the introduction of her replacement.

The new *Saint Eloi* was named after the city of Dunkirk's patron saint and following the liquidation of her Italian builders, she was subsequently very late in delivery. The unfinished ship was seized by her creditors and laid up in the port of Genoa and eventually took up service some 39 months late in March 1975.

During March 1977, ALA was wholly taken over by BR although the French company continued to exist as a subsidiary of the British Railways Board.

With the 'Night Ferry' through sleeping car service between London and Paris/ Brussels being axed in October 1980, the Dunkirk train ferry service was gradually downgraded. It became freight only in 1985 and in preparation for SNCF's super-train ferry, the *Nord Pas-de-Calais*, the old train ferry

SNCF introduced the second ***Cote d'Azur*** from Le Havre builders following war losses in 1951. The turbine steamer was forever associated with the Calais-Folkestone link and is seen to full advantage arriving at the British port, her sleek lines amply illustrating that she was capable of making 25 knots. *(FotoFlite)*

dock at Dover was finally closed in May 1988 with SNCF's *Saint-Germain* passing for scrap shortly afterwards. The *Saint Eloi* meanwhile was chartered to SNCF for the summer train-connected service between Dover and Calais but with a Calais-based crew, she became the subject of many complaints and was less than a success. After a winter period relieving on the Irish Sea, in 1989 she was renamed *Channel Entente* and once more adopted a Dunkirk-based crew.

Following the ship's sale to the Isle of Man Steam Packet Company two years later, the SNCF vessel *Chartres* was chartered and wore the ALA funnel colours for her daily seasonal Dover-Calais train-connected services until it ceased in September 1993 after which the ship was sold to Greek owners.

SNCF – FRENCH NATIONAL RAILWAYS

Apart from their vessels in the Newhaven-Dieppe joint fleet, the Société Nationale des Chemins de fer Francaise (SNCF) also operated ships from Calais and Dunkirk. In order to replace two

ships which were lost during hostilities, SNCF supplied the diesel train ferry *Saint-Germain* and the turbine passenger steamer *Cote d'Azur* which both entered service in 1951. Train ferry expertise was then very much in Denmark and the 'Germain' was built at Elsinore, appearing with the Danish signature drop of hull paint below the bridge. She was a huge improvement on the original trio of Swan Hunter & Wigham Richardson built steamers and gave SNCF a 25 per cent share in the Dunkirk route. The second vessel took over the Calais-Folkestone service from BR's *Canterbury* and very much made it her own during the rest of her 21-year career with occasional early morning peak weekend sailings to Dover.

It was not until 1958 that the car ferry *Compiegne* was introduced on the Calais-Dover link where she competed for the seasonal traffic with Townsend's converted frigate *Halladale*. Technically the new Rouen-built ferry represented a huge advance on anything yet seen in the English Channel and she was very much a trendsetter. Not only was she fitted with controllable-pitch propellers, which the Captain could operate

The ***Compiegne*** was the first car ferry built in France and joined the Calais-Dover service in June 1958. The ship introduced a number of technical innovations which became the norm in vehicle ferry construction, notably controllable pitch propellers which could be actioned directly from the bridge rather than via the engine room in addition to bow-thrust units. *(Michael Woodland)*

The train ferry **Saint-Germain** was a product of the Elsinore Shipyard in Denmark and joined the Dunkirk-Dover link in July 1951 thereby giving SNCF a 25 per cent share in the route. This reliable vessel continued in service until 1987. *(Michael Woodland)*

directly from the bridge without the delay of passing through the engine room, but she was also built of all-welded construction and also introduced a stern-docking bridge. With capacity for 164 cars on three levels, additionally she carried 1,000 one-class passengers and early in her career was regularly used on the Calais-Folkestone passenger service when the Cote d'Azur was off for her annual winter overhaul. Delays at the shipyard saw the Saint-Germain start the SNCF car ferry service until 18th July when the new ship took up service operating thrice daily.

A long-awaited second car ferry was the Nantes-built Chantilly (210 cars, 1,200 passengers) which also boasted a number of new features – a nursery for mothers and children, an escalator from her car decks into the passenger areas and closed-circuit television showing films in some of her lounges. After trials at Calais, Boulogne and Newhaven, the new ship entered service in June 1966 right in the middle of the major NUS strike and was pressed into service a week early in order to relieve her hard worked fleet companion.

In 1970, BR came to an agreement with their French trading partners that would involve them being able to use the 'Sealink' brand name and thus they are included in this book.

During the winter of 1969-1970, the Compiegne was sent to Le Havre where her after end was raised by 56cm in order to accommodate more freight vehicles. She remained a stern loader but the Chantilly was converted to drive-through following her own major surgery in 1976.

At the close of September 1972, SNCF withdrew their Cote d'Azur from service and purchased the Normannia for a year until such time that their new multi-purpose ferry Chartres was introduced. The Normannia raised the tricolor and was re-registered in Calais, working with a French crew for the duration. The ship was returned to the red ensign during October 1973 while the new Chartres entered service on the Dunkirk train ferry

The car ferry **Chantilly** entered service between Calais and Dover in June 1966 but during the winter of 1974/75 was converted to drive-through operations. Here she is at Calais loading vehicles in readiness for an afternoon sailing to Dover. *(John Hendy)*

Left: The *Compiegne* is seen leaving Dover Eastern Docks later in her career and after her stern was raised in order to accommodate extra freight vehicles (notice the rise in windows below the third lifeboat). *(Ken Larwood)*

Below: The *Chantilly* is seen arriving at Folkestone before her conversion to drive-through operations. She was unusual having stern doors which opened horizontally rather than vertically. Dover's Admiralty Pier can be seen in the far distance. *(Bruce Peter collection)*

Bottom left: The train ferry *Saint-Germain* is seen later in her career with the 'Sealink' legend applied to her hull and with 'SNCF' on her red funnel. *(Michael Woodland)*

Bottom right: During 1974, the SNCF freight vessel *Transcontainer I* of 1968 had rails added to her lower vehicle deck which allowed her to operate the Dunkirk train ferry both to Harwich and to Dover. In 1985, the vessel was moved to Dieppe for an unsuccessful service to Portsmouth. *(Michael Woodland)*

The first of the three Dover-Dunkirk train ferries to be built was the **Twickenham Ferry** which was handed over to the Southern Railway's French subsidiary ALA prior to the service opening in October 1936. Affectionately known by the French as 'Le Twick', the steamer was the last of the trio in service due to the delayed arrival of her Italian-built successor. *(Don Smith/Phototransport.com)*

Between the departure of the passenger steamer **Cote d'Azur** in 1972 and the arrival of the new multi-purpose vessel **Chartres** in 1974, SNCF were a ship short and so it was arranged for the **Normannia** to be transferred to SNCF control for that period. Here she is flying the tricolor and registered in Calais departing from Dover on a morning sailing to Calais. *(Michael Woodland)*

The much delayed **Saint Eloi** finally joined the Dunkirk-Dover train ferry service in March 1975, a whole 39 months late after her Italian builders were declared insolvent and she was seized by her creditors in Genoa. *(FotoFlite)*

The third **Cote d'Azur** (later renamed **SeaFrance Renoir**) entered service between Calais and Dover in October 1981. She is seen arriving at Folkestone for trials prior to entering service as the **Horsa** heads away to Boulogne. *(FotoFlite)*

The **Londres** was ordered before the outbreak of war but was seized on the stocks by the invading German army. She finally entered service between Dieppe and Newhaven in April 1947 but following the withdrawal of the British-crewed **Worthing** in 1955, was transferred to British ownership and registry. Her sister ship **Arromanches** remained under SNCF control. *(John Hendy collection)*

Dieppe's **Lisieux** entered service to Newhaven in 1953 and remained in service after the conversion of the route to car ferry operation in 1964. For the 1965 season she was chartered to French Lines (CGT) for excursions from Torquay and Weymouth to the Channel Islands, during which time she wore a red funnel. She was not a success and the 12 year old steamer was subsequently sold to Greek owners. *(Ken Larwood)*

Above: The ***Villandry*** was the first of a pair of car ferries which entered service for SNCF on the Dieppe-Newhaven route in 1965. Both ships were converted to drive-through operations in 1976 and 1977. *(FotoFlite)*

Left: During her final four seasons in service, the ***Chartres*** was chartered by Sealink UK's French subsidiary ALA to operate summer train-connected sailings between Dover Western Docks and Calais Maritime. This time-honoured service ceased in September 1993 after which the ship was sold to Greece. *((FotoFlite)*

Below: Between 1982 and 1990 the ***Chartres*** was based at Dieppe although made two brief winter sorties back to the Dover Strait to give winter cover on the Dunkirk train ferry link. *(FotoFlite)*

The 1947-built **Koning Albert** is seen coming astern into Dover at the conclusion of her 3 hour 20 minute crossing from Ostend as SNCF's **Compiegne** arrives off the port from Calais. *(AG Jones/ John Hendy collection)*

link in the following February.

As with BR's *Vortigern*, the *Chartres* was built to operate as a train ferry during the winter months and switch to the intensively operated car ferry links during the summer. In order to fit the confines of Dover's train ferry dock, her hull was almost identical to that of the *Vortigern* as was that of the later ALA train ferry *Saint Eloi*. However, the demand for vehicle space was increasingly acute and both the *Vortigern* and the *Chartres* were to spend increasingly lengthy periods working in that role. Between 1982 and 1990, the French vessel was switched to the Dieppe station which effectively kept the ageing *Saint-Germain* in service at Dunkirk for another five years until she was withdrawn in 1987. The *Chartres* was replaced in service at Calais by the first of a new generation of French ferries, the third named *Cote d'Azur*.

A further SNCF vessel to see service on the Dunkirk West-Dover link was their ro-ro/ train ferry *Transcontainer 1* which had been built at La Seyne during 1968. After operating between Dunkirk and Harwich, rails were fitted to her vehicle deck in 1974 for train ferry work between Dunkirk to Harwich and Dover. In 1975 she inaugurated a service from Dunkirk to Felixstowe which continued until April 1984 when she was transferred to the Dieppe station.

The French contribution to Sealink's 'Flagship Service' was the splendid Le Havre-built *Cote d'Azur* which entered service in early October 1981, the same month in which the *Compiegne* left Calais for the final time for Greek owners. With accommodation for as many as 330 cars or 43 pieces of freight and 1,400 passengers, the new ship quite outshone her twin British running partners both in aesthetic terms and also in her vastly superior passenger spaces.

Following the departure of the BR steamer *Caledonian Princess* at the end of the 1981 season, SNCF's *Chantilly* was rostered to operate the train-connected services in 1982 but was not a success. With the new *Champs Elysees* entering service in October 1984, shortly afterwards the small *Chantilly*

was moved to the Dieppe-Newhaven link for the remainder of her career. The *Champs Elysees* boasted capacity for 300 cars, 54 freight units and as many as 1,800 passengers making her the largest Sealink ferry in the Dover Strait. Her on-board facilities represented an improvement over the *Cote d'Azur* and, as has been related elsewhere, unsuccessful efforts were made to recapture the Dover-Boulogne market.

Following the de-nationalisation of Sealink UK Ltd in July 1984, the new owners Sea Containers attempted to purchase SNCF Armement Naval but due to intense pressure from the French seamen's unions, they were ultimately unsuccessful.

After Sea Containers had lost a hostile takeover bid from the Swedish Stena Line in May 1990, relationships between SNCF and the Swedes rapidly deteriorated and the cultural gulf between the companies widened until a split became inevitable. On New Year's Day 1996, an independent SeaFrance was born and the close co-operation and groundwork laid by the nationalised railway concerns of Britain and France was torn up.

BELGIAN MARINE ADMINISTRATION/ REGIE VOOR MARITIEM TRANSPORT

With the new twice-nightly car ferry service from Folkestone to Ostend due to commence in July 1972, at which time BR would gain a 15 per cent share of the route, in November 1970 the Belgian Marine Administration joined the Sealink consortium. In the following year the Belgian Government's shipping arm modified its name to Regie voor Maritiem Transport (RMT) and in 1973 the unhappy-looking company monogram began to appear on the funnels of the Ostend-Dover fleet.

In 1970, the Belgian cross-Channel fleet consisted of the six passenger/ mail vessels *Koning Albert* and *Prince Philippe* (of 1947 and 1948), *Roi Leopold III*, *Koningin Elizabeth* and *Reine Astrid* (1956, 1957 and 1958) and the *Prinses Paola* which was built as late as 1966. The mail boats were timed to complete the 62-mile passage in 3 hours 20 minutes and were two-class

Above: Ostend Quay with the 1958 car ferry ***Artevelde*** unloading after her arrival from Dover Eastern Docks with the ***Princesse Astrid*** (1968) in the adjacent berth. *(August Goethals collection)*

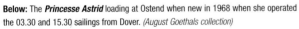

Below: The ***Princesse Astrid*** loading at Ostend when new in 1968 when she operated the 03.30 and 15.30 sailings from Dover. *(August Goethals collection)*

Below: The ***Roi Leopold III*** is seen leaving Ostend Quay for Dover. *(August Goethals collection)*

The first of three identical passenger vessels built in time for the Brussels Universal Exhibition of 1958 was the **Roi Leopold III**, a product of the Cockerill yard in 1956. These handsome ships were laid aside during the 1970s particularly after the linkspan was opened on the Admiralty Pier in 1974 allowing the car ferries to carry train-connected passengers. *(Dom Smith/Phototransport.com)*

vessels. They were each able to accommodate some 30 crane loaded cars in their holds and even carried the occasional coach on their poop decks. The five-strong one-class car ferry fleet comprised the 90-car *Prinses Josephine-Charlotte* (ex *Car Ferry*) of 1949, *Artevelde* (1958), *Koningin Fabiola* (1962), *Roi Baudouin* (1965) and *Princesse Astrid* (1968). The later car ferries each carried 160 cars and crossings were scheduled to take 3 hours 45 minutes. In addition there was the little used cargo vessel *Ijzer* of 1954 which was eventually disposed of in 1972.

In spite of huge opposition from Ostend, Townsend Car Ferries opened up a new service from Dover to Zeebrugge in March 1966 and rapidly developed the blossoming roll on-roll off freight market. At the same time, the Belgian Marine fleet was aesthetically a delight to the eye and wholly traditional in nature, reflecting the traffic of an earlier and largely bygone era. If the Belgian fleet were to compete with Townsend then a complete rethink was necessary.

The arrival of the *Princesse Astrid* in August 1968 was to coincide with the opening of a new five-hour link between Ostend and Harwich which was commenced by the *Roi Baudouin* in late May. The lack of advance bookings was disappointing, the route failed to capture the public's imagination and the service was eventually closed in September 1973.

The first of a new generation of car ferries entered service in July 1973. The *Prins Philippe* replaced the passenger vessel of the same name which had been chartered for use in the Baltic where having survived an engine room explosion, she was gutted by fire at Mariehamn. The new ferry was the first to appear with the RMT monogram on her funnel and with the word 'Sealink' along her hull. Costing £5 million, the ship carried 1,240 passengers, 243 cars and was the line's first drive-through vessel. Although representing a tremendous advance on the previous Ostend ships, her fixed mezzanine decks limited the amount of freight she could carry and her career was limited

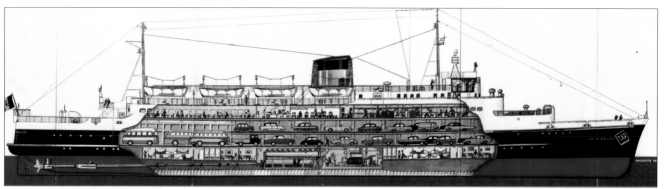

A publicity image produced by Belgian Marine (later RMT) prior to the introduction into service of the **Artevelde** in 1958. The layout was simple and well tried in the days before high-headroomed freight vehicles were carried by sea. *(August Goethals collection)*

Top: The Ostend route proved to be so popular with foot passengers that even as late as 1966, the splendid *Prinses Paola* was required for the train-connected services. The last of her breed ever built for UK services, the ship remained in service until September 1987. *(John Hendy collection)*

Above left: The time-honoured method of carrying vehicles across the Channel is exemplified in this image as a car is lifted by crane into the *Car Ferry* which loaded in this manner at Dover's Admiralty Pier until the Eastern Docks Terminal was opened in June 1953. *(August Goethals collection)*

Above right: High density seating of the railway carriage variety was fitted into all the passenger vessels. Here is the *Prinses Paola*. *(August Goethals collection)*

Left: The huge volumes of passengers' luggage were lifted in nets and later metal trolleys into the ships' holds. The passengers streaming on board the *Reine Astrid* do so across open quaysides which afford little protection in inclement weather. *(Bruce Peter collection)*

The new RMT livery certainly did nothing to enhance the looks of the Belgian fleet. Here is the by now rarely used **Koningin Elizabeth** (of 1957) leaving Dover at Easter 1977. *(John Hendy)*

Off service at Ostend in 1968 are the **Prince Philippe** of 1948 and the **Prins Albert** of 1937 both of which were latterly used on the Folkestone-Ostend service. These ships epitomised the post-war Belgian Marine fleet prior to its inclusion in the Sealink consortium. *(John Hendy)*

The original two berths at Dover Eastern Docks are occupied by the British Rail turbine steamer *Lord Warden* and the Belgian vessel *Roi Baudouin* which is seen on her arrival from Ostend with her bow rudder in use. *(John Hendy)*

The *Roi Baudouin* as she looked in her full RMT livery. As with all Ostend ships of the period, she displayed beautiful lines but the advent of the roll on-roll off revolution demanded a radical rethink in ferry design which the Belgians were slow to adopt. *(FotoFlite)*

Above: The *Artevelde* of 1958 leaving Dover for Ostend late in her career. After a charter to Sealink UK's Dover-Calais service vice the late *Earl Leofric* in 1976 as with many of her fleet contemporaries she passed for further trading in Greece. *(Don Smith/Phototransport.com)*

Left: In a bid to improve their freight-carrying capacity, RMT's final ships were a far cry from those introduced in the 1960s. Here is the *Prinses Maria-Esmeralda* leaving Dover's Admiralty Pier berth. In 1985/86 both she and her sister were cut in half horizontally when an extra freight deck was added increasing their capacity from 46 to 55 lorries. *(Don Smith/Phototransport.com)*

Bottom left: By 1981, RMT had retained only two conventional passenger vessels, the oldest of which was the *Reine Astrid* of 1958. She bowed out at the close of the season and was converted to become the new jetfoil terminal at Dover. *(John Hendy collection)*

Below: The new vehicle ferry linkspan on Dover's Admiralty Pier was opened in June 1974 and allowed car ferries to carry the still significant numbers of rail-connected passengers. Here we see the *Prince Laurent*. *(Jim Ashby)*

The first of the new generation of Belgian ships was the unsuccessful ***Prins Philippe*** of 1973. Although a limited amount of freight could be accommodated, she was built with fixed mezzanine decks which hampered her flexibility. In 1985 she was chartered to Sealink UK for the Weymouth-Cherbourg link where she proved to be a great success largely carrying tourist cars. *(Ken Larwood)*

to just 13 years. However, her sister ship *Prince Laurent* was built without mezzanine decks and although car capacity was sacrificed, she could carry 24 lorries as opposed to her sister's 13. The 'Laurent' entered service in June 1974 and opened the new linkspan on Dover's Admiralty Pier at the Western Docks. Its construction was to have a significant effect on the traditional passenger ship fleet as vehicle ferries were now able to carry train-connected passengers directly to Dover's Marine Station. The line's centenary vessel *Koning Albert* (1947) finished service in October 1973.

A third multi-purpose vessel was the £8 million *Prinses Maria-Esmeralda* which boasted capacity for 1,200 passengers, 300 cars or 37 lorries and 46 cars. Entering service in May 1975, she was followed by the *Princesse Marie-Christine* in late

December. There now followed a huge exodus of the traditional fleet with the *Roi Leopold III* and *Koningin Elizabeth* becoming Red Sea pilgrim carriers while the car ferries *Prinses Josephine-Charlotte* and *Artevelde* both sailed for further careers in the Greek islands. By the end of 1976, it was announced that freight traffic on the Ostend route had risen by 13 per cent.

A third and slightly modified member of the 'PME' class entered service in March 1978. This was the *Prins Albert* which was the final Belgian cross-Channel vessel to be built at the famous Cockerill yard at Hoboken.

Twin Boeing jetfoils were introduced in May and July 1981 on an impressive 100-minute schedule. The *Princesse Clementine* and *Prinses Stephanie* carried 273 passengers at speeds of up to 42 knots at a time when one-third of all people

Beauty and the Beast? This view sums up the gulf that existed within the RMT fleet in July 1983. The final passenger vessel ***Prinses Paola*** arrives from Dover while the box-like second ***Reine Astrid*** (ex ***Stena Nautica***) loads vehicles for her evening departure. The former Stena Line ship was purchased from Canadian owners in February 1983 having entered service at Ostend in the previous April. *(John Hendy)*

In a further bid to increase freight capacity, RMT took a three-year charter of the Yugoslav-built **Stena Nordica** (later renamed **Stena Nautica**) from Stena Line. Following her charter, she passed to SNCF and became their **Versailles** on the Dieppe-Newhaven link before briefly becoming the **SeaFrance Monet** at Calais. *(John Hendy)*

The **Prinses Maria-Esmeralda** in her stretched form which required large stability blisters welded to her hull. *(FotoFlite)*

In May 1981 RMT introduced the **Princesse Clementine** on their 100-minute fast passenger service between Ostend Quay and Dover Marine. Operated by a pair of 42-knot Boeing jetfoils, the craft proved to be extremely popular if extremely expensive to operate. Here is the second of the twins, **Prinses Stephanie** being named at Ostend prior to her introduction in July. *(August Goethals collection)*

The first of RMT's jetfoils, the **Princesse Clementine**, is seen arriving at her home port in July 1983. *(John Hendy)*

using the Ostend-Dover link were still classified as foot passengers (i.e. without cars).

The penultimate passenger vessel *Reine Astrid* finished service in October 1981 and was converted to become the new jetfoil terminal at Dover, a role which commenced during June 1983.

More freight space was created with the charter of the Stena Line vessel *Stena Nautica* in April 1982. Capable of carrying 43 lorries, the ship was purchased in February of the following year and renamed *Reine Astrid*. A further Stena charter took place in May 1983 when the *Stena Nordica* was taken on a three-year bareboat charter. Entering service in the following month, in March 1984 she was renamed *Stena Nautica.*

After brief charters to Sealink UK Ltd, both the car ferries *Roi Baudouin* and *Princesse Astrid* sailed for Greece in 1983. They were joined by the remaining early generation car ferry *Koningin Fabiola* which most unusually had undergone a mini-conversion during the winter of 1976-77. At this time her upper vehicle deck was converted to passenger lounges thus increasing her passenger capacity from 850 to 1,200 and reducing her car spaces from 160 to 88. In this role she proved useful doubling up on the summer service from Dover's Western Docks but this was the only instance of a vehicle ferry conversion to create extra passenger space at the expense of a car-carrying capability.

All three of the 'PME' class were next for attention during 1985-86 when they were sliced horizontally and had an extra vehicle deck inserted thus raising their lorry space from 46 to 55 pieces of freight but by the time that the *Prins Albert* had reappeared during May 1986, the Sealink connection was dead.

When in July 1984, Sea Containers had purchased Sealink UK Ltd, the new owners immediately began a reappraisal of all their services. Included in their master plan was a scheme to increase their 15 per cent share of revenues on the Ostend link to 50 per cent and accordingly the *St David* was switched to

Dover from the Irish Sea in March 1985.

This proved to be too much for the Belgians who now did the unthinkable and entered into negotiations with their arch rivals Townsend Thoresen. The joint service commenced on New Year's Day 1986 and effectively prohibited Sealink British Ferries from operating to Belgium.

Once again the well-tried and well-laid plans which had been honed by state-owned operators over many years' mutual respect and understanding had been undone by new owners adopting aggressive and wholly unacceptable commercial pressures. Understandably, these proved to be totally abhorrent to Sealink's continental partners.

POSTSCRIPT

RMT's agreement with Townsend Thoresen allowed the British company to take as much as 63 per cent of all freight revenues and looking for a fairer balance, in 1994 RMT became partners of Sally Line and switched their UK base to Ramsgate. By making the move, the Belgians effectively committed commercial suicide and the historic service was wound up just three years later.

SMZ (STOOMVAART MAATSCHAPPIJ ZEELAND)

The ships of the Zeeland Steamship Company (SMZ) had successfully operated the daylight service between the Hook of Holland and Harwich since 1946. Originally based at Vlissingen, the port and its surrounding infrastructure were so badly damaged during the war that it was inevitable that the Dutch ships should move to duplicate the route then served by the London & North Eastern Railway's overnight fleet.

Close co-operation between SMZ and British Rail was cemented when in 1966 they announced that their services were to be reorganised and that each was to build a new car ferry. The SMZ contribution to the new service was the Cammell Laird built *Koningin Juliana* (1,200 passengers, 220 cars) which

The ***Koningin Emma*** leaving Harwich for the Hook of Holland. *(Ferry Publications Library)*

Left: Passengers board the **Koningin Emma** at the Hook; a miserable experience on a wet and windy day. *(Bruce Peter collection)*

Below left: Entrance foyer on the **Koningin Emma** . *(Bruce Peter collection)*

Bottom left: The promenade deck on board the **Koningin Emma**. Deck loungers give the impression of a cruise, but on a wild night on the North Sea this deck would take on a very different appearance. *(Bruce Peter collection)*

Bottom right: The **Koningin Emma** . *(Bruce Peter collection)*

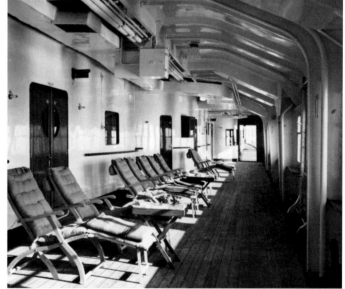

Above: Outward bound in the River Stour, the interesting-looking *Koningin Wilhelmina* sails for the Hook of Holland. *(John Hendy)*

Left: The handsome *Prinses Beatrix* of 1978. *(Bruce Peter collection)*

Below: The *Koningin Juliana* arrives at Harwich. *(Bruce Peter collection)*

The **Koningin Juliana** was modelled on British Rail's **St George**, but with much finer lines. *(FotoFlite)*

was delayed from entering service following a fire during her fitting-out period. She eventually took up station operating night crossings with BR's *St George* during October 1968. At this time the traditional passenger vessels, SMZ's pre-war diesel sisters *Koningin Emma* and *Prinses Beatrix* and BR's post-war steamer *Arnhem* were withdrawn. The passenger vessels *Amsterdam* and SMZ's *Koningin Wilhelmina* were retained for daytime sailings as BR's *Avalon* was on charter and not available.

Vibration problems with the *St George* saw the diminutive *Normannia* and then Holyhead's *Hibernia* assisting during the autumn before the fully integrated service commenced in November at which time the *Amsterdam* was withdrawn. The remaining steamer was the *Avalon* but her days were numbered when the new *St Edmund* was ordered in 1970. On her entry into service the 11 year old *Avalon* was sent for conversion to a car ferry for the Fishguard station.

The centenary of SMZ was marked in 1975 and three years later the Dutch company introduced the splendid new *Prinses Beatrix* which entered service in June 1978 replacing the route's final passenger-only vessel the *Koningin Wilhelmina.* The new ship boasted capacity for 1,500 passengers and 320 cars.

With four vehicle ferries now on the North Sea link, the smaller original pair doubled up sailings, the 'George' working in partnership with the 'Beatrix' operating overnight from Harwich with the 'Edmund' and the 'Juliana' leaving Harwich every morning.

The requisitioning of the *St Edmund* for the Falkland's War in 1982 severely stretched the service and SMZ chartered the DFDS vessel *Prinz Oberon* which had been spare ever since closing the Harwich-Bremerhaven service.

Sealink UK's charter of Stena Line's spare *Prinsessan Birgitta* replaced both British ships and as the *St Nicholas*, she took up service in June 1983. It was now time for SMZ to re-evaluate its own service and it was decided that one large ship should replace the two existing vessels. In 1985, a new £40 million ferry was duly ordered from Van der Giessen-de-Noord but during April 1984, SMZ chartered the Larvik-Frederikshavn Line's *Peter Wessel* which they renamed *Zeeland* to replace the *Koningin Juliana* which sailed to her new Italian owners. In October 1985, the *Prinses Beatrix* was sold to Brittany Ferries and chartered back until April 1986 while during March and April 1986, SMZ briefly chartered the French company's *Armorique* to replace the *Zeeland*.

The new super-ferry was the *Koningin Beatrix* which appeared with an all-white hull without 'Sealink' along her. The new ship entered service during April 1986 and offered capacity for 2,100 passengers and 485 cars.

In 1998 the Dutch Minister of Transport announced that the Government were to sell its controlling interest in SMZ and although Sealink British Ferries were one of four prospective purchasers, the Swedish Stena Line were eventually successful. On 22nd June 1989, Stena took control thereby ending the 114 years of SMZ's involvement in North Sea operations.

Sealink
and before

CHAPTER FIVE

Isle of Wight

On New Year's Day 1948, the British Transport Commission's Isle of Wight services inherited three quite diverse crossings with totally different requirements.

The Portsmouth-Ryde link was by far the most important of the services being train connected on both sides of Spithead. Serving a population largely without their own means of transport, the route's passenger steamers were at their busiest on summer Saturday mornings during the weekly exodus to and from the mainland. At these times, huge queues of holidaymakers, each encumbered with a week's worth of luggage, would arrive by train at Portsmouth Harbour or Ryde Pier Head stations awaiting passage. On the Island side, huge queues, many deep, would snake back down Ryde Pier towards the Esplanade. Throughout the early 1950s, it was usual to see in excess of 40,000 passengers using the service on August Saturdays.

The fleet was composed entirely of coal-burning paddle steamers which included the elderly *Shanklin* (1924), *Merstone* (1928), *Whippingham* (1930) and the sisters *Sandown* (1934) and *Ryde* (1937). The largest of these vessels was the *Whippingham* which had (with her sister *Southsea* – a war loss) operated popular pre-war excursions around the Isle of Wight and further afield. At the end of hostilities, these outings were limited to within the Solent area and the more elderly fleet units would see little service outside the summer peak season. Throughout the period under review, the numbers of foot passengers using the route both rapidly and markedly declined so that by the time of writing (2015), just two 260-seater catamarans are employed to cope with the traffic on offer.

The second of the three Isle of Wight routes was the car ferry link between Portsmouth (Broad Street) and the remote village of Fishbourne, a few miles to the west of Ryde. The Southern Railway had transferred this service from George Street Slipway at Ryde in March 1926, initially using the time-honoured 'horse-boats' pulled by tugs but in 1927 they introduced the revolutionary car ferry *Fishbourne* (15 cars) which was followed in 1928 and 1931 by the modified sister ships *Wootton* (16 cars) and *Hilsea* (17 cars). Although double-ended vessels, they were always used as single enders but represented a huge improvement on the very basic service they had replaced. However, it is important to stress that the service was provided for motorists and foot passengers were not encouraged.

Whereas the Ryde route has declined in importance throughout the years, the car ferry route has grown out of all

A product of the Caledon yard at Dundee in 1928, the **Merstone** is seen arriving at Ryde in July 1945 still painted in her wartime grey livery. Her starboard paddle digs deep as passengers ready themselves for disembarkation. *(Bert Moody)*

The end of the **Whippingham** as she is towed out of Portsmouth Harbour on her way to the breakers in Belgium on 17th May 1963. *(Terry Creswell collection)*

The **Sandown** was built by Denny's at Dumbarton and joined the service in June 1934. *(AE Glen/ Bruce Peter collection)*

proportion and Fishbourne has very much superseded its neighbour as the premier gateway to the Isle of Wight.

The Lymington-Yarmouth crossing was and is the shortest of the three routes to the Isle of Wight and was again different in that Lymington was train connected via a branch line from Brockenhurst and until September 1953, Yarmouth too boasted a railway station. Cars had been carried (via specially adapted barges) from an early time and in 1938 the Southern Railway had introduced the dual-purpose *Lymington* (20 cars, 430 passengers) to transport both cars and foot passengers across the Western Solent. One of the last ferries ordered by the Southern Railway was the diesel electric paddle vessel *Farringford* (32 cars, 320 passengers) which eventually took up service for her new owners in March 1948. The 1948 fleet was completed with the coal-fired paddle steamer *Freshwater* (1927) – 500 passengers – which were discharged at the end of Yarmouth Pier rather than at the slipway used by the car ferries. The ship's use was very much of a seasonal nature and mainly catered for the large numbers of tourists that descended on West Wight's holiday camps. The new *Farringford* replaced the ancient paddle steamer *Solent* (of 1902) in the Lymington fleet.

Retained in local service during the war, she was finally retired in 1947 before her sale in September of the following year which meant that she was never to operate for the nationalised railway company.

PORTSMOUTH-RYDE

In order to replace its two war losses (*Portsdown* and *Southsea*), the Southern Railway had ordered two quite revolutionary vessels for the Portsmouth-Ryde service. The twin-screw motor vessels *Southsea* and *Brading* were launched at Denny's Dumbarton yard within 30 minutes of each other on 11th March 1948. Each costing in the region of £160,000, the twins had a length of 200ft with a beam of 47ft. Passenger certificates for as many as 1,331 in two classes were to make them the largest ships ever built for the route and throughout their long careers, they proved to be the most successful ships ever to serve it. Their twin eight-cylinder diesel, non-reversible Sulzer engines drove them at 14 knots.

Entering service on 1st November and 2nd December 1948, the new ships were immediately popular and with the benefit of the magic eye of radar, were able to maintain the

The ancient **Solent** was built for the Lymington-Yarmouth link at Southampton in 1902 and although withdrawn from service in 1947, she was not broken up until the following year in BR ownership. *(AE Glen/ Bruce Peter collection)*

Lymington-Yarmouth's **Freshwater** was the route's final paddle steamer, having been built at Cowes (Isle of Wight) in 1927. Attempts to keep her running in private ownership failed and she was broken up in 1962. *(Tom Rayner)*

island lifeline even in the thickest of fogs. A third, similar, sister was ordered and the *Shanklin* took up station on 18th June 1951 replacing the paddle steamer of the same name which was sold to Cosens of Weymouth and survived another ten years as their *Monarch*. The new *Shanklin* was a one-class ship from the outset and the Portsmouth-Ryde service became single class from that day. The vessel had a rather larger funnel than her two sisters which always made her look more imposing and was also improved, from a passenger's viewpoint, by having her lifeboats raised above the deck thereby offering unobstructed all round views of the passage. Mechanically though she was not quite as versatile as her sisters. As an economy measure her gear-boxes and clutches were dispensed with, the engines being made reversible and connected directly to the propeller shafts. The *Shanklin* remained the preferred mid-week cruise vessel throughout her

career although her outings were usually limited to viewing the liners at Southampton Docks.

The *Merstone* was retired in September 1952 leaving the service in the hands of the three new diesel vessels and the trio of 1930s paddle steamers. The next to go was the coal-hungry *Whippingham* which finished service in September 1962. Good to the last, on her final day in service she shipped over 7,000 passengers to and from the island.

Towards the end of 1964, the new face of British Rail was launched to an unsuspecting public. The shipping division's black hulls became blue, funnels were changed to red with the new BR logo while initially, upperworks became grey. For the Isle of Wight services the new livery was trialled on the *Brading* which reappeared with her hull paint raised to the level of her Promenade Deck. Such was the public outcry that it was not long before the blue paint was again lowered a deck.

The last paddle steamer in operation to the Isle of Wight was the Denny of Dumbarton built **Ryde** of 1937. She is seen moored off Portsmouth Harbour station in June 1966 ready to take up afternoon sailings from the Southsea piers to Ryde. *(John Hendy)*

The *Sandown* was to last just one more season in her new livery before being towed away for scrapping in Belgium thereby leaving the *Ryde* as the Solent's final paddle steamer. Her role by this time was to maintain the Southsea-Ryde link, helping out on the principal Portsmouth-Ryde service on Saturday mornings from late May until September. However, on 13th September 1969, she was eventually withdrawn from service and the Southsea calls were terminated although the following year saw the reintroduction of Portsmouth-Southsea (Clarence Pier)-Ryde services. The ship was sold to become a floating 'boatel' at Island Harbour, between East Cowes and Newport on the Isle of Wight where she joined the paddle steamer *Medway Queen*. Much has happened to her since then, including a serious fire in 1977, but having been abandoned for more years than she was in service, her rusting and collapsing hulk is today a very sad sight.

The three diesel ferries had received long-overdue refits in 1967 when a Spar Deck was added with seats for 170 passengers. In order to lift the diesel fumes clear of the new passenger decks, both the *Southsea* and *Brading* were fitted with stove-pipes to their funnels which were later hidden when their funnel rims were eventually extended. Internal changes included the resiting of the cafeteria and a major seating upgrade. Further work to the accommodation, costing £100,000 per ship, was carried out at Immingham during 1973/74.

The British Rail subsidiary Seaspeed was formed in March 1966 and within months the company was operating ferry services within the Solent area. Initially this involved the operation of twin SRN-6 hovercraft between Southampton and Cowes and later Portsmouth and Cowes. In early 1968 a third route was tried from Portsmouth to Ryde firstly using an SRN-6 before on 1st April, a 65-seater Hovermarine HM-2 took over. The early service proved to be most unreliable although the 1969 summer season showed 15 weekday ten-minute crossings between Portsmouth and Ryde. As the craft became more reliable, British Rail were confidently to announce that their five-year plan included replacing the diesel ferries with the new generation of high-speed craft. However, the Seaspeed service finally folded in September 1972 although the local management had obviously gained much useful experience during the previous six years.

Although more money was later spent on the *Shanklin* to make her more suitable for cruising, she now began to suffer from annoying engine problems and it was decided to withdraw her in March 1980. With only two ships now left in service, the decision was taken to axe both the mid-week cruises and all calls at Clarence Pier, Southsea. During the same month that the *Shanklin* was withdrawn, British Rail took on charter the Western Ferries high-speed catamaran *Highland Seabird* for a week of trials during peak periods.

As for the *Shanklin*, she was sold for just £25,000 during October to supporters of the preserved Scottish paddle steamer *Waverley*. The faulty engine problems were rectified and as the *Prince Ivanhoe*, she was introduced for a summer season's cruises in the Bristol Channel. On 3rd August 1981, she hit an underwater obstruction off the Gower peninsula and was tragically lost.

During the final nationalised years, plans were in hand to replace the elderly diesel twins with high-speed Norwegian-built catamarans, each capable of carrying 500 passengers. The craft would make the crossing in ten minutes and were expected to enter service during 1983. However, it was now decided that due to the expenditure on the Fishbourne route, any fast craft would have to await Sealink's forthcoming privatisation. A token fast craft was introduced during summer 1983 (August-September) with the charter of the 85-seater Vosper Hovermarine HM-218 SES (GH 2094) *Ryde Rapide*. The vessel mainly operated between Southsea (Clarence Pier) and Ryde but the experiment was not repeated.

So at the age of 36 years, the *Southsea* and *Brading* were returned to private ownership when in July 1984, Sealink UK Ltd was passed to the Bermuda-based Sea Containers. Ordered by the Southern Railway, they had survived throughout the entire nationalised era and were undoubtedly the most successful and reliable ships that the route has ever seen.

PORTSMOUTH-FISHBOURNE

The nationalised years of the Isle of Wight services were to see a total re-emphasis in traffic trends. As car ownership grew

Seen on passage across Spithead in her original form is the **Brading**, the second of a trio of highly successful diesel ferries each of which was capable of carrying over 1,300 passengers. Withdrawn in 1986, the vessel was broken up at Portsmouth eight years later after a failed preservation attempt. *(FotoFlite)*

Above: The revolutionary *Fishbourne* of 1927 was the first of the Isle of Wight car ferries. The punt-like vessel is seen leaving the original Broad Street slipway en route for the Island and could accommodate just 16 vehicles. *(John Faulkner collection)*

Left: The *Lymington* of 1938 was the first car ferry on the Yarmouth service. Fitted with Voith-Schneider propulsion, the ship proved to be highly manoeuvrable and was not sold out of service until 1973. *(John Hendy)*

Below: The *Farringford* was driven by independent diesel electric paddle wheels. She joined the Lymington station in 1947 and was also retired in 1973 after which she was switched to the Hull-New Holland ferry service for which she served as a side loader until its closure in 1981. *(John Hendy)*

The third Lymington car ferry was the **Freshwater** of 1959. A product of the Ailsa yard at Troon, she could carry 26 cars and was replaced in 1983 after which she served for Western Ferries in Scotland for a further 12 years. *(John Hendy)*

in the 1960s and rail travel declined, the numbers of holidaymakers using the traditional link between Portsmouth and Ryde dramatically declined in favour of the car ferry service to Fishbourne.

Throughout the 50s, the three ageing car ferries were becoming increasingly capacity constrained and it came as no surprise that in November 1958, British Railways announced modernisation plans for the route.

Originally to be named *Fishbourne* and *Wootton*, the first-generation vessels were given the suffix 'II' so as to free the names for the new ships. However, at some later stage during the construction process, it was decided that the second ship should have a name associated with the mainland port of departure and as the terminal was in a dock called the Camber, the name *Camber Queen* was clumsily adopted.

The two new ships, each costing £175,000, were ordered from the Philip & Son yard at Dartmouth. Capable of accommodating as many as 34 cars and 168 passengers they boasted very spartan accommodation with passenger lounges below car deck level, one of which was fitted with a refreshment kiosk. Most passengers opted to remain in their cars for the passage and the crews frequently earned extra money by offering to wash their vehicles. Management turned a blind eye to such practices!

Mechanically, the vessels were fitted with Voith-Schneider propellers which became the standard fixture on all subsequent car ferries. With a speed of 10.5 knots, they could accomplish the crossing in about 35 minutes as opposed to the 55 minutes

of their predecessors.

The *Fishbourne* and *Camber Queen* were rather odd-looking vessels with staggered deckhouses either side of a central bridge. This was in order to accommodate large transporter lorries which it was anticipated would carry aircraft bodies from the Saunders Roe works at East Cowes. With this traffic in mind, the ships were given a high vehicle deck headroom of 15ft but the traffic failed to materialise and so the ships' design was never fully tested.

In order to accommodate the new ships, a new terminal with wider slipways and its own car park was opened in the Camber at Broad Street and a new terminal building came into use in July 1961. At Fishbourne too, a new slipway was built at right angles to the original thus allowing easier access from the approach channel as it faced the sea and not Wootton Creek. Nearby, a large car park was constructed as part of the £1 million reorganisation programme.

The *Fishbourne* was the first to enter service on 7th July 1961 (replacing the ship of the same name) and was followed by the *Camber Queen* on 29th August. The old *Wootton II* and *Hilsea* finally finished service in September and October and all three original car ferries were later sold to Harry Pound's scrap yard up at the north end of Portsmouth Harbour. The *Wootton II* was soon broken up in the Netherlands but the other two were resold to the Dutch Oil Company who used them to ferry heavy drilling materials to the island of Terschelling. They were finally scrapped in 1967.

The two modern ships quickly began to generate extra

The original trio of car ferries on the Portsmouth-Fishbourne route were replaced during 1961 by the Dartmouth-built twins **Fishbourne** (pictured) and **Camber Queen**. The twins boasted accommodation for 168 passengers and 34 cars and remained in service until 1983. *(John Hendy*

holiday traffic while commercial traffic also showed healthy growth. By the late 60s this had grown to such an extent that the first of a third generation of Isle of Wight car ferries was ordered from the Richards' yard at Lowestoft. What became the *Cuthred* was quite unlike anything previously seen with her passenger accommodation right across the vehicle deck offering far more in the way of comfort and facilities. She was also the first local ferry to be given a name associated with the Dark Ages which was by then the BR naming policy for all their ships.

The *Cuthred* took up service on 9th July 1969 and boasted increased capacity for 400 passengers and 48 cars although the fitting of a mezzanine deck during the late 70s, increased this number by 24.

Further expansion of the Fishbourne route came in 1973 when the first of a trio of sister ships entered service from the Robb Caledon yard at Dundee. The *Caedmon* was in every way an improved *Cuthred*, her more powerful engines and larger diameter propellers making her an altogether more successful ship. Car capacity was for as many as 52 while up to 750

The underpowered **Cuthred** was the first of a new generation of car ferries with greater headroom for freight and improved passenger facilities. She entered service in July 1969 and was sold in 1987. *(John Hendy)*

Above: The *Brading* is seen approaching Portsmouth following the addition of her upper Spar Deck and internal modifications in 1967. The subsequent raising of her funnel rim greatly improved her looks. Along with her sister ship, she served throughout the entire period of nationalised ownership. *(Kenny Whyte)*

Left: The *Shanklin* was the most attractive of the three post-war diesel ferries having raised lifeboats and a larger funnel. Her entry into service in June 1951 introduced one-class travel on the Portsmouth-Ryde route. Sold out of service with engine troubles in 1980, she became the *Prince Ivanhoe* but was tragically lost off the Gower in the following year. *(Don Smith/Phototransport.com)*

Below: The *Southsea* was the first of the trio of post-war motor ships, entering service in November 1948. Finally retired in 1988, after a two-year stint as an excursion ship, she was eventually purchased for preservation but was scrapped in 2005. Her funnel stove-pipes were added after her 1967 modifications and were eventually hidden by the raising of the funnel rim. *(AG Jones)*

passengers could be carried. Her twin sisters were intended for the Lymington station and during November, the third of the class, the *Cenred*, stood in on the Fishbourne link for two months before taking up station there. The installation of mezzanine decks later increased car capacity to 76.

But demand for vehicle space on the Portsmouth-Fishbourne link was insatiable and a complete re-evaluation of the basic design of ferry was now required. Capacity problems at Portsmouth's Broad Street terminal were solved by the acquisition of the redundant Gunwharf site that duly opened for use on 21st February 1982. The old slipway method of loading was dispensed with as linkspan operation was introduced on both sides of the Solent. Slipways had served the service well using smaller vessels but there was always the risk of becoming stranded on a falling tide which could not only prove to be a major inconvenience but also risk damaging the ships' Voith Schneider propellers. With plans in the air to replace the 1961 twins with larger vessels, the switch to linkspan loading was seen as essential.

The fourth generation ships, *St Catherine* and *St Helen* were built at Henry Robb's yard at Leith and introduced a completely new concept in travel to the Island. The £5 million *St Catherine* entered service on 3rd July 1983 and was followed by her sister on 28th November. They totally eclipsed the vessels that they replaced and with accommodation for as many as 1,000 passengers and 142 cars (88 on the Main Deck and a further 54 on the mezzanine), 24 commercial vehicles could be carried on the Main Deck if required. Both ships briefly appeared in the traditional BR livery but in preparation for the privatisation of Sealink UK Ltd, without the company's double arrow logo on their funnels.

The *Camber Queen* was sold in January 1984 and sailed to Portugal where, as the *Mira Troia*, she was to operate the 2.5 mile Setubal-Troia route for another 14 years. The *Fishbourne* was mechanically the poorer of the twins but after being sold to HG Pound's scrap yard up at the top of Portsmouth Harbour,

was repurchased by interests representing the Turkish Republic of Northern Cyprus for a totally unsuitable 125-mile service to southern Turkey. Eight months later, as the *Kibris I*, she was swamped at her moorings in a gale and was lost.

With the two new ships in service at Portsmouth, the *Caedmon* was duly moved to the Western Solent to operate the Lymington-Yarmouth link with her sisters while the *Cuthred* was relegated to seasonal and relief work.

LYMINGTON-YARMOUTH

Although the shortest of the three railway-operated routes to the Isle of Wight, the Lymington-Yarmouth crossing has always been extremely demanding. The meandering confines of the Lymington River in addition to the strong tidal flows sweeping through the Needles Channel and into the Western Solent have always demanded both powerful and highly manoeuvrable ships.

Three months after the formation of the British Transport Commission in January 1948, the route received the services of the new diesel electric paddle vessel *Farringford* from Denny's Dumbarton yard and her partnership with the *Lymington* of 1938 was to continue until 1973. The earlier vessel was fitted with Voith Schneider propulsion units but in view of the then problems in obtaining spare parts from Germany, it was decided to fit her with independently operated paddle wheels propelled by diesel electric engines and, as such, she was very much a 'one off' within her sphere of operation. Overall the system worked well although she always lacked the manoeuvrability of the earlier vessel.

By 1955, some 42,000 cars a year were being shipped on the route which resulted in an order for a third car ferry. This was a new *Freshwater* which was built by Ailsa at Troon and which entered service on 21st September 1959. Capable of carrying 620 passengers and 26 cars, she replaced the paddle steamer of 1927 which had been renamed *Freshwater II* in readiness for her arrival. The steamer was later purchased for excursion work,

The **Caedmon** was the first of a trio of identical ships built by Robb Caledon at Dundee and entered service at Portsmouth in 1973. Ten years later she was switched to the Lymington station where she joined her twin sister ships. All three were withdrawn in 2009 and scrapped in Denmark. *(FotoFlite)*

The **St Catherine** was added to the Portsmouth fleet in July 1983 and was so successful that she was later joined by three more sisters, the latter two of the series being added during private ownership. Original accommodation was for as many as 1,000 passengers and 142 cars. She was withdrawn in 2009, her sister ship **St Helen** following her to Sardinian operators in 2015. *(John Hendy)*

running as the *Sussex Queen* from Brighton and then the *Swanage Queen* for work in the Swanage/ Bournemouth area before passing to Belgian breakers in May 1962.

With as many as 109,000 cars using the crossing in 1967, plans were announced for larger ships. The first of the trio (*Caedmon*) was destined for the Portsmouth route but the *Cenwulf* and *Cenred* would replace the *Lymington* and *Farringford*. The first of the new Lymington vessels made her maiden voyage on 18th October 1973 and was joined by the *Cenred* in the following January after serving a period of relief at Portsmouth. Both the smaller vessels were withdrawn during November, the *Lymington* becoming the *Sound of Sanda* for Western Ferries on the Clyde while the *Farringford* was adapted to operate the Humber ferry between Hull and New Holland. The *Freshwater* continued to act as relief ship until she too was replaced in 1983 when the *Caedmon* was released from Portsmouth to operate with her two sister ships. She was then sold to HG Pound for scrapping at Portsmouth but eventually followed the old *Lymington* into the Western Ferries fleet where she became their *Sound of Seil*. Curiously, after the opening of the Humber Bridge, the *Farringford* was also purchased by Western Ferries although she never operated for them, being broken up at Hull in 1984. After being withdrawn in 1989, the former *Lymington* was again sold in 1994 and reduced to a hulk in connection with a fish farm on Loch Etive while the ex *Freshwater* remained in service on the Clyde until 1995 after which time she passed to a Garston breaker for conversion to a crane barge. Shortly afterwards the company went into receivership and the remains of the ship were simply abandoned on the banks of the Mersey.

POST 1984

Sealink UK Ltd was de-nationalised in 1984 and taken over by Sea Containers of Bermuda after which time the fleet traded as Sealink British Ferries. Then in 1990, the Swedish company Stena Line seized control but Sea Containers retained the Isle of Wight services which were renamed Wightlink. The name was retained after CINVen Ltd, a venture capital company, acquired the business in 1995 and then following a management buy-out in 2001. In 2005, Wightlink was purchased by the Macquarie

Group of Sydney, Australia; and again in 2015 when it was further sold to Balfour Beatty Infrastructure Partners.

PORTSMOUTH-RYDE

The *Brading* and *Southsea* were eventually replaced by twin catamarans in 1987, the *Brading* being withdrawn after a series of mechanical problems during February. There were a number of plans to preserve her but eventually she passed to HG Pound's scrap yard at Portsmouth where she was broken up in 1994. The *Southsea* was retained in service both to assist on the ferry link on Saturday mornings and also to run cruises during the summer seasons of 1987 and 1988 after which she also was withdrawn and laid up. Her demise was far more protracted and could well form the subject of a book. Suffice to say that all valiant attempts to save her for preservation failed and she was scrapped at Esbjerg (Denmark) in 2005; 57 years after first entering service. The replacement catamarans lasted for 19 and 22 years.

PORTSMOUTH-FISHBOURNE

The *Cuthred* was withdrawn from service in January 1987 and after a long lay-up followed by a brief sojourn on the Tyne (where it was planned to convert her into a Mississippi stern-wheel style restaurant), in 1990 she passed to the same Portuguese owners as the *Camber Queen*. She was renamed *Mira Praia* and was finally laid aside in 2009.

The first of the fourth-generation ferries *St Catherine* was withdrawn in 2009 and sold to the Italian company Delcomar for service in Sardinia where she was renamed *GB Conte*. Sister ship *St Helen* followed her as the *Anna Mur* in 2015. The initial pair were joined by two more sisters: the *St Cecilia* and *St Faith* were introduced for Sealink British Ferries in 1987 and 1990 while a larger Polish-built double-decked ferry *St Clare* joined the newly named Wightlink fleet in 2001.

LYMINGTON-YARMOUTH

All three 1973 sisters, *Caedmon*, *Cenwulf* and *Cenred* were replaced by three new Croatian-built sisters (*Wight Light*, *Wight Sky* and *Wight Sun*) in 2009 and were subsequently sold for scrapping at Esbjerg (Denmark).

The Irish shipping services of the former LMS and GWR came under British Transport Commission control managed regionally by the new British Railways. At Stranraer, services came under the new Scottish Region, the London Midland Region covered Heysham and Holyhead. At Fishguard, the GWR's share in the Fishguard & Rosslare Railways & Harbours Co. was transferred to the Western Region, but this was moved again to the London Midland Region in 1952.

The post-war recovery and increasing prosperity of the British nation brought to many people for the first time the possibility of travel to the continent. In Ireland it was a different matter and while the shipping services there had been travelled by generations of Irish migrants, the economic reconstruction of England after the Second World War saw many Irish people leave home, some never to return. Recruitment campaigns by employers such as the National Health Service and London Transport were designed to address severe labour shortages. Some of these campaigns were directed specifically at Ireland, where unemployment was high and the standard of living was generally lower than in Britain.

In particular, services at Holyhead and Fishguard made London more accessible for Irish migrants than before the war. As well as providing young Irish people with better employment prospects, London also offered them the opportunity to widen their social circle.

In the immediate period post nationalisation the British Railways fleet serving its Irish routes consisted of ageing tonnage on one hand and new state of the art ships on the other. At Fishguard, the new Rosslare ship *St David* had just entered service alongside the *St Andrew* of 1932 and on the link with Waterford, the cargo-passenger steamer *Great Western*, built in 1934. Ordered to the GWR's specification the *St David* was built to a design little changed from pre-war days and was greatly inferior to the two new London Midland motorships that appeared at Holyhead just one year later, the *Hibernia* and *Cambria*. The Dun Laoghaire service at that time was also home to the *Princess Maud*, which then became third ship on the link and Irish Sea relief vessel. The 'Maud' was built for Stranraer in 1934 and served with distinction during the war. Holyhead also offered nightly cargo/cattle services to Dublin and a weekly service to Greenore, operated by the *Slieve Bawn*, *Slieve League*, *Slieve Bloom*, *Slieve More* and the *Slieve Donard*.

At Heysham the overnight Belfast crossing was served by three 1928-built sisters, the *Duke of Lancaster*, *Duke of Rothesay* and *Duke of Argyll*. A fourth 'Duke', the *Duke of York*, was transferred to the Harwich-Hook of Holland service early in 1949. Heysham had to wait until 1956 before it saw three new passenger ships. Cargo services at Heysham were also operated by the *Slieve Bearnagh* and the *Slieve Bloom* which could each carry about 700 head of cattle in addition to general cargo.

In the north, following the departure of the *Princess Maud* to Holyhead, Stranraer had the *Princess Margaret* and the new car ferry *Princess Victoria*. The latter was a replacement for an almost identical ship of the same name, lost to a mine off the Humber in 1940. She had been Britain's first specially built stern-loading car ferry and at the time represented a huge leap in ferry design.

It must be said that the railways always put the best of everything into their vessels and these old ships had been very

The **Duke of Argyll** of 1928. Fast packets of 3,600 gross tons, the 'Argyll' and her sisters, the **Duke of Lancaster** and the **Duke of Rothesay**, could carry 1,500 passengers with sleeping berths for 454. In addition, they had space for around 500 tons of cargo and about 250 cattle. *(Bruce Peter collection)*

advanced in the 1930s. For example, the *Princess Maud* was the first British-flag ship to have automatic fire sprinklers. But by the late 1950s and into the 1960s they were well past their prime with spartan accommodation for passengers and crew alike. When compared against the English Channel the Irish services were also a late starter in the car ferry arena. For the Caledonian Steam Packet's (CSP) Stranraer-Larne service across the Irish Sea, a splendid new stern-loading steam turbine-powered ferry, the *Caledonian Princess*, was ordered from Wm Denny & Bros of Dumbarton for delivery in 1961.

Her arrival was the catalyst for a new wave of tonnage but even then British Rail was slow to develop the market. Holyhead received the *Holyhead Ferry I* in 1965, but the car ferry service remained a seasonal affair for ten years. At Fishguard, it wasn't until 1972 that a full ro-ro service was offered and this after a line of ad hoc side-loading conversions.

By now air travel was becoming a force to be reckoned with and even before the advent of the low-cost operating model, airlines were attracting large volumes of classic passenger traffic that would have otherwise opted for ship and rail.

One must not forget the cargo services maintained by quite a substantial fleet of ships. In 1956 livestock accounted for almost 35 per cent of Ireland's total exports. British Railways routes from Heysham, Holyhead and Fishguard handled some 37 per cent of this livestock trade. Shortly after nationalisation, closed containers for the shipment of perishable goods were introduced. Up to 60 small containers of four tons with capacities ranging from 500 to 700 cu. ft could be shipped on the cargo/cattle boats at any one time.

FISHGUARD

Car traffic on the Rosslare service began its rapid growth in

1961 when daylight sailings were introduced two days a week during the summer months. Traffic levels had grown so much by 1963 that British Railways took the decision to convert the *St David* to a side-loading car ferry in time for the summer season. The resulting improvements certainly provided for a better level of service, but the whole affair had something of a Heath Robinson feel about it. At Rosslare Pier, cars had to board railway flats for the short trip to Rosslare Mainland as there was no road to the berth! In that first season as a car ferry the *St David* carried 20,000 cars. Car traffic soon outgrew capacity and in 1966 a most unusual solution was put in hand with Holyhead's cargo ship, the *Slieve Donard*, being allocated to the run for the summer months. Equipped with a stern door, the Holyhead ship accommodated cars while their drivers and passengers crossed in the *St Andrew*.

Complaints were high and again questions were asked in Dáil Éireann.

Mr Lalor, Parliamentary Secretary to the Minister for Transport and Power and Posts and Telegraphs: "I understand that there were some complaints about the service provided for the transport of cars and passengers on the Rosslare-Fishguard route during the 1966 tourist season. British Railways have informed me that these complaints arose from the fact that they were unsuccessful in chartering a suitable drive-on/drive-off car and passenger ship to augment the two regular vessels on the route during the 1966 season".

The *Duke of Rothesay*, a modern stabiliser-equipped vessel, is being adapted to provide side-loading drive-on/drive-off facilities for 112 cars and will have ample cabins/berths/seating accommodation for 1,400 passengers with lounge, cafeteria and bar facilities, first and second class. The *Duke of Rothesay*, operating in conjunction with the *St David*, will provide an increase of approximately 30 per cent on the car capacity of the Rosslare-Fishguard route for the 1967 season, with drive-on/drive-off facilities on both vessels."

The arrival of the larger ship brought the withdrawal of the *St Andrew* which was sold for breaking up in Antwerp by Jos. De Smedt. Two years later the *St David* left Fishguard for the last time and after service at Holyhead and Heysham was sold to Chandris Cruises. Renamed *Holyhead* the ship sailed to Greece in 1970, however she was destined to never see service there and was eventually broken up.

Meanwhile, the *Great Western* was withdrawn from service in January 1967, being replaced initially by the chartered *Eden Fisher*. During her annual overhaul in April 1959 the *Great Western*'s second-class accommodation for 320 passengers was removed and the resulting space aft used for the shipment of containers. The remaining first-class accommodation was given over to crew use and in June passengers ceased to be carried. Before sailing for Belgium and the breakers yard, the ship spent two months operating between Heysham and Belfast in place of the *Slieve Bearnagh*.

An interesting proposal arose in 1968 following the termination of B+I Line's Cork link with Fishguard in favour of Swansea, a decision imposed on the Irish company by British Rail who regarded their proposed new car ferry service as an 'unfriendly act'! This brought the end of direct rail-connected services and pending delivery of the new *Innisfallen*, Cork was left with no regular passenger service to Britain. Such was the local anger at losing the service, albeit temporarily, that a committee of Cork citizens sought to charter the North Sea passenger vessel *Avalon* from British Rail for one round passenger voyage from Fishguard to Cork on 23rd December, returning to Fishguard on 25th December. The proposal was cancelled at the 11th hour due to a lack of support.

For the 1969 summer season the *Duke of Rothesay* was joined by the *Caledonian Princess*. Side-loading doors were cut into the side of the Stranraer ship and such was the success of the new addition that the two-ship operation was repeated in 1970 and in the following year the 'Caley P' officially became a Fishguard ship.

Fishguard finally received a full drive-on/drive-off service on 6th July 1972 when the port's new linkspan was opened for business by the *Caledonian Princess*. Car and truck traffic surged ahead and in 1973 the German ro-ro cargo vessel *Neckartal* was chartered to supplement car ferry sailings. Her sister *Isartal* was chartered in 1974 and renamed *Preseli* but by now it was known that the *Caledonian Princess* was spending

her final year on the route as British Rail was turning one-time pride of the fleet, the former Harwich passenger vessel *Avalon*, into a stern-loading car ferry for the service.

The *Caledonian Princess*'s final crossing was from Rosslare on the morning of 19th June 1975, after which she destored and transferred to the Channel Islands services. The *Avalon* made her debut on 15th July 1975, however, despite being a Fishguard ship she also spent much time at Holyhead, perhaps illustrating the long held local perception that the Pembrokeshire operation was somewhat inferior to those in the north.

During 1977 British Rail announced their intention to close the Waterford container with effect from 18th March 1978, because of the losses being incurred. Since the late 1960s the service had been operated at various times by the Container Enterprise, *Container Venturer* and the *Isle of Ely*.

An interesting cross-pollination of routes was trialled in 1978 when the veteran car ferry *Lord Warden* opened a new summer service from Fishguard to Dun Laoghaire. With a crossing time of 5 hours and 30 minutes the service was not a great success and despite initial intentions to run it again in 1979 the route failed to reappear, most likely due to the introduction of the newly acquired Swedish ferry *Stena Normandica* as a replacement for the *Avalon*. Overnight, the route saw quite a boom in freight traffic but this was brought to an abrupt halt when in June the new addition suffered major engine trouble. In a freight-only mode she continued to operate on one engine until 23rd July when she was withdrawn for attention at Holyhead. Two months passed before the *Stena Normandica* returned to service.

The original intention was for the 'Normandica' to remain at Fishguard until the arrival of a new-build in 1980, but in the event the *St David* was switched to Holyhead when the chartered vessel proved to be a considerable success. The chartered ship was eventually purchased by Sealink British Ferries in April 1985 and renamed *St Brendan*.

HOLYHEAD

The arrival of the new motor ships in 1949 fulfilled a pre-war proposal to replace the 1920-built ships of the same name with two turbine steamers from the Clyde yard of Fairfield Shipbuilding & Engineering Co. Ltd, an order subsequently cancelled due to the onset of war. After the war, British Railways turned to Harland & Wolff at Belfast for the two ships and the first of these, the *Hibernia*, arrived in Holyhead for the first time on 5th April 1949 to a huge welcome from locals and dignitaries, including Lady Megan Lloyd George.

Under the command of Captain Albert Marsh, the *Hibernia* entered service on 14th April. The *Cambria* was brought out by Captain W.H. Hughes arriving at Holyhead from Belfast on 5th May. The old *Hibernia* and *Cambria* were withdrawn from service in December 1948 and May 1949 respectively and were broken up at Barrow and Milford Haven. The regular pattern for the mailboats was for one nightly sailing in each direction on a year-round basis. This was increased by a second sailing in each direction during the summer months with a third at peak periods taken by the *Princess Maud*. Additionally, a very popular *Princess Maud* sailing was the 'North Wales Excursion' when she sailed from Holyhead to Dun Laoghaire at 09.00 with day-trippers from holiday resorts along the coast brought to the shipside by train.

One benefit of nationalisation was a significant increase in work for the local marine workshops. Holyhead boasted extensive facilities to maintain its not inconsiderable fleet of

The Fishguard & Rosslare Railways and Harbours Co's **St Andrew** gets underway for Wales. Unlike the rest of the British Railways fleet, the **St Andrew** and her Fishguard companions retained the GWR livery of black-topped red funnel while flying the Fishguard and Rosslare house flag. She continued in railway service until 1967 when she was broken up. *(David Heath)*

Above: The *Cambria* slips into the River Lagan from Harland & Wolff's Belfast shipyard at Queen's Island. Over in the fit-out berth is sister ship *Hibernia* while across the river is one of the pre-war Heysham 'Dukes' and the cattle boat *Slieve Bearnagh*. The *Hibernia* and the *Cambria* entered service at Holyhead in April and May 1949 respectively and were the mainstays of the Dun Laoghaire service for over a quarter of a century. *(Jim Ashby collection)*

Left top: The *Great Western* on Waterford's River Suir. Entering service at Fishguard in 1934 this handsome little GWR ship carried the buff funnel colours of British Railways unlike the black-topped red-funnelled passenger ships at Fishguard. She lasted long enough to wear the new British Rail livery introduced in 1965. *(John Hendy collection)*

Below: In steam at Larne is the *Princess Margaret*. This ship dated from 1931 and 20 years later was dispatched to Glasgow for conversion from coal to oil burning. As such she saw another ten years' service at Stranraer before being sold for further duty in Hong Kong. After facing all that the Irish Sea weather could hurl at her, she succumbed to a typhoon in 1971. *(John Hendy collection)*

Once the pride of the British Railways fleet, the **Avalon** at Fishguard following her conversion to a stern-loading car ferry. On taking up service at the Welsh port in 1975 she was the largest Sealink ship in Irish operation but despite this, having been downgraded to relief status at Holyhead, she was sold for scrap just five years later. There was no place for fuel-thirsty turbine steamers in the new age of double deck ro-ro ferries. *(John Hendy collection)*

ships and now, under the new regime, all Irish Sea, North Channel and St George's Channel ships were dry-docked and refitted at the port. On occasion ships from the English Channel were also regular visitors to the larger of the two dry docks.

Relief ships occasionally appeared, most notably the *St Patrick* in 1950 and 1951, and also the *Duke of York* and from the Channel Islands, the *Isle of Sark*. Before the end of the decade, the Isle of Man Steam Packet Company's *Snaefell* was hurriedly chartered by British Railways to replace the *Cambria* on 12th August 1959. Leaving Douglas at 19.00, she arrived at Dun Laoghaire four hours later and sailed again for Holyhead at 23.30.

Dominating the development of Holyhead's services in the post-war era were the changes in the mode of travel with the rise of the motorcar, containerisation and decline of passenger rail traffic, resulting in the closure of the Station Hotel in 1955.

With the new efficiencies of containerisation the weekly cargo Greenore service was discontinued in 1951 followed in 1954 by the withdrawal of the elderly *Slieve Donard*. By this time the *Slieve Bawn* was spending long periods in service at Heysham with the *Slieve Bearnagh*.

The *Slieve Bloom* was the first of the cattle boat quartet to see withdrawal and in 1965 she and the *Slieve More* were sold to Van Heyghen Freres for breaking up in Belgium. The *Slieve Bawn* was moved back to Holyhead and shortly afterwards Associated Humber Lines' *Harrogate* was transferred to the port, entering Irish Sea service on 15th April 1965. Her sisters, the *Selby* and the *Darlington*, became frequent visitors, assisting when traffic demanded additional capacity.

Holyhead's first car ferry was ordered in 1963 and to facilitate the new vessel extensive engineering works were put in hand on both sides of the Irish Sea. The opening of the service in 1965 fell to the *Normannia*, hastily brought around from Dover when the new *Holyhead Ferry I* was delayed at her builders. The service got underway on 9th July with the new ship taking up the run on 19th July. Accommodation was provided for 1,000 passengers with space for 153 cars on the vehicle deck. During the height of the summer season, one round trip was offered daily. At weekends an additional round trip was offered. The whole operation was a most civilised affair.

Cabins for the 06.00 sailing from Dun Laoghaire were available for occupation overnight. Although a huge success, the car ferry service was seasonal and on 17th October the route reverted to mailboat operation until the summer of 1966.

The arrival of the *Holyhead Ferry I* brought the withdrawal of the *Princess Maud*, her final sailing being from Dun Laoghaire on 4th September 1965. She was quickly sold for Greek service and as she left the Welsh port for the last time one of the marine yard fitters, Wesley Williams, who was an accomplished bugler, played 'The Last Post' as she steamed past the Refit Berth on her way to warmer climes. She was finally broken up in Spain in 1973.

The *Slieve League* followed her sisters to the breakers in February 1967, leaving the *Slieve Bawn* as the last of the 'old boats'. International Standards Organisation (ISO) 20-foot containers were shipped through Holyhead for the first time on 2nd January 1968. In preparation for this the *Harrogate* and the *Selby* were both converted to cellular container ships and these maintained services pending delivery in 1970 of two purpose-built cellular container ships from Verolme Dockyard in Cork, the *Brian Boroime* and the *Rhodri Mawr*.

The new container operation was brought to an abrupt halt when Robert Stephenson's Britannia Bridge across the Menai Strait was virtually destroyed in a fire on 23rd May, severing Anglesey's rail link with the mainland. The decision was taken to transfer the ISO service and the mailboats to Heysham, the former running to Belfast. With a crossing time of 7 hours and 30 minutes, the *Hibernia* and the *Cambria* continued to sail from the Lancashire port to Dun Laoghaire until 31st January 1972 when they were welcomed back to Holyhead with a fireworks display.

Shortly after the fire a new service between Heysham and Dun Laoghaire was opened using the *Holyhead Ferry I* and the *Dover*. Commencing on 27th June 1970 the seasonal service was operated by the Holyhead ships in addition to their regular sailings. Departures were offered from the Irish port on Tuesdays, Thursdays and Saturdays, sailing at 08.00 and arriving in Heysham at 14.50 before returning two hours later with an arrival in Dun Laoghaire at 22.40. The season ran until 19th September and was repeated again in 1971. Increasing traffic at Holyhead brought the venture to an end and it failed to return in 1972.

The end of the Dublin livestock service came in 1975 and the last remaining cattle boat, the *Slieve Donard*, left Holyhead for the final time, under tow, on 1st July, bound for the Red Sea via Birkenhead. The cargo service was now purely ISO but the future, however, was truck traffic and container volumes on British Rail's final Irish Sea lift-on/lift-off service between Holyhead and Belfast/Dublin were being adversely affected by the early 1980s.

In March of that year an order was placed with Aalborg Vaerft A/S in Denmark for a new ship to replace the mailboats and the *Holyhead Ferry I*. The end of the time-honoured mail service came with the last sailing of the *Cambria* on 7th September. On the following day the ship stood down and the *Holyhead Ferry I* launched the new year-round multi-purpose service. Under the command of Captain Ivor Griffiths the *Cambria* slipped out of Holyhead for the final time at 23.00 on 28th October. She arrived at Barrow at 09.00 the following morning and remained there until sold to Orri Navigation of Saudi Arabia in January 1976. Renamed *Al Taif*, she sank while at anchor in Suez Roads in January 1981.

The *Hibernia* remained on the Holyhead link until 3rd October 1976 when she arrived at her home port with her final sailing from Dun Laoghaire. After sale to Agapitos Brothers of Greece she was renamed *Express Apollon*. On 18th December 1980 she was observed at Bombay and four weeks later she was at Darukhana in India where Solid Steel Traders began demolition. As for the *Holyhead Ferry I*, as an official Dover ship she was sent in 1976 to Swan Hunter on the Tyne for conversion to drive-through operation – a configuration she should have offered when built. She emerged renamed *Earl Leofric*.

Taking up commercial service on 2nd May 1977 the new *St Columba* was an overnight success on the Dun Laoghaire route. With capacity for 2,400 passengers, 335 cars or 36 artics, this massive new ship changed the entire profile of this key Irish Sea route. Effectively replacing three ships after just one year in operation she had carried her one-millionth passenger. She was a much needed breath of fresh air on the crossing which, since the withdrawal of the mailboats, had been operated by a variety of stop-gap steam turbine car ferries,

The **Slieve More** was one of five 'Slieve' boats running between Holyhead, Dublin and Greenore when the railways were nationalised. Built in 1932 she had a speed of around 17 knots and could carry in the area of 650 head of fat cattle and 538 tons of cargo. *(Charles Brinsley Sheridan/Justin Merrigan collection)*

including the *Duke of Lancaster*, the *Duke of Rothesay*, the *Duke of Argyll*, the *Caledonian Princess*, the *Avalon* and the *Dover*.

Each summer a second ship was deployed to augment the *St Columba*. From time to time the *Avalon*, *Lord Warden* and *Duke of Lancaster* plus the ro-ro vessels *Dalriada*, *Transbaltica* and *Stena Timer* all partnered the crack ship until in 1981 a newcomer arrived in the camp fresh from Harland & Wolff – the *St David*.

Post privatisation the prime Holyhead services went through many highs and lows including the loss of its second ship. Under Stena Line stewardship it not only regained a second ship, but did so on a year-round basis. The route was selected for the company's first high-speed experiment culminating in the introduction of the first HSS vessel in 1996. But by 2013, while ro-pax services into Dublin Port had developed, the Dun Laoghaire operation had dropped from five round trips to one round trip per day between March and September with additional sailings operated over the Christmas and New Year period until services to Dun Laoghaire ceased in 2014.

HEYSHAM

The pre-war passenger ships were replaced in 1956 by three new steamers of the same names, the first of which to enter service was the *Duke of Lancaster*. She differed slightly internally from the others as she was completed with off-season cruising in mind. Her first cruise came in June 1958, sailing from

In her final year of service the **Hibernia** goes astern at Holyhead. Defaced by the Sealink legend on her monastral blue hull, this was the end of the fabled Holyhead mailboat service; the car ferries had taken over. *(Don Smith/Phototransport.com)*

A splendid view of the new **St Columba** nearing the end of her delivery voyage from Aalborg to Holyhead on 5th April 1977. This massive new ship had 2,700 seats for 2,400 passengers, guaranteeing every passenger an undercover seat. Winter 1982 saw the conversion of the ship from two class to one class and what was to be the first of a number of alterations to her comfortable accommodation, culminating in a rebuild by Sealink Stena Line in 1991 from which she emerged as the **Stena Hibernia**. *(Justin Merrigan collection)*

Southampton for Amsterdam, Ostend and Rouen. Subsequent cruises brought her to Scotland, Denmark, Norway and Spain and until 1966 up to six cruises a year were the norm.

Two new cargo ships, the *Container Enterprise* and the *Container Venturer*, were introduced in 1958, the very first British Railways ships specially designed for carrying containers.

While the *Duke of Rothesay* underwent conversion to a side-loading car ferry for Fishguard, the remaining two ships were converted to stern-loading vehicle carriers in 1970. The *Duke of Argyll* opened the new car ferry service with her overnight sailing from Belfast on 24th February. In her new guise, the ship offered space on her two metres clear height vehicle deck for 105 cars, although just inside the stern door there was room on the centreline for two coaches. Up top, gone was the traditional two-class accommodation for 1,800 passengers; one class for 1,400 passengers was now the order

of the day.

Sailings were offered six nights a week, stepping up to seven nights during the summer. During peak periods daylight crossings were also made. By 1973, however, the Belfast crossing was in real trouble, the political situation in Northern Ireland having played its part. In an attempt to revive interest in the service First Class facilities were reintroduced, having been dispensed with when the ships were converted. But the rot had set in and talk of closure stalked the crews. Talk became reality and in March 1975 it was announced that the route would close on 7th April. In the event, the last car ferry sailing was two days earlier with the *Duke of Argyll*'s sailing to Belfast and the *Duke of Lancaster*'s crossing to Belfast.

A freight-only ro-ro service was introduced in partnership with P&O utilising the *Penda* and later the *Dalriada*. P&O withdrew from the arrangement and in a last ditch effort to make

The **Holyhead Ferry I** comes astern onto the ramp at Holyhead's Admiralty Pier in 1965. The car ferry service was a huge success but even so it was still a seasonal affair until 1975. *(Justin Merrigan collection)*

Seen from the **St Columba** on the Refit Berth, the **St David** arrives at Holyhead from Dun Laoghaire. Originally planned for the Fishguard to Rosslare service, the **St David** was instead allocated to Holyhead replacing the **Avalon** as the second ship. *(Captain Neville Lester)*

Built in 1959 by Ailsa Shipbuilding at Troon the general cargo and cattle ship **Slieve Donard** was unusual in that she had a stern door to allow up to 61 cars to be driven onto the main deck. She could accommodate 150 cars in all, usually trade cars, but normally she carried up to 668 head of cattle or 30 x 20ft containers, or an equivalent mix of each. Thanks to her drive-on, drive-off capabilities the ship quite often saw supplementary service at Stranraer and Fishguard during the summer months, carrying additional cars while drivers and passengers travelled on the principal ships. *(Bruce Peter collection)*

the route pay two chartered ships, the *Lagan Bridge* and the *Lune Bridge*, were introduced in 1980. By the end of the year the ships were gone and the route closed.

In August 1978 a newcomer appeared in the Heysham camp in the form of Manx Line and their *Manx Viking*, introducing a full ro-ro service to the Isle of Man for the first time.

A series of incidents, including breakdowns and storm damage, all conspired against the fledgling company. Struggling with financial difficulties Manx Line was rescued by British Rail (60 per cent) and James Fishers (40 per cent). By 1981 the company was being marketed under the Sealink brand name and on 16th April that year the *Manx Viking* returned to service from annual overhaul in full Sealink colours, apart from the Manx Three Legs of Mann symbol on her funnels.

Following the 1985 merger between the Isle of Man Steam Packet Company and Sealink the *Manx Viking* returned to Douglas from overhaul in the former's colours. This was to be her final year on the Irish Sea and at the end of September 1985 she slipped away from Douglas for the last time.

STRANRAER

The new *Princess Victoria* was practically identical in all respects to her lost 1939 namesake, notwithstanding the fact that eight years had elapsed. While representing another instance of stagnation in Scottish short-sea ship design, she was, however, a Sulzer-engined motor ship and therefore considerably more up to date in terms of propulsion than, for example, the post-war *Waverley*.

The British seamen's strike of 1966 caused the suspension of British Rail's shipping services and here, from the right, we see the **Duke of Rothesay** and the **Duke of Lancaster** along with the **Selby** laid up at Heysham. On 23rd May, a week after the outbreak of the strike, the Government declared a state of emergency, although emergency powers were not used. The strike finally came to an end on 1st July. *(John Pryce collection)*

Above: The **Duke of Argyll** laid up for sale at the end of her railway career. As the **Zenith** this once proud ship was gutted by fire at Hong Kong in 1995. *(Bruce Peter collection)*

Left: The **Container Enterprise** in dry dock at Holyhead. A huge range of skilled work was carried out by engineers and craftsmen of all trades at the port's marine workshops. Other railway ports made good use of the dry dock for their ships but by the early 1980s ferries being built were on a much larger scale and had outgrown the Holyhead facility. In 1986 the dry dock was closed and eventually infilled to provide extra standage at the port. *(A.G. Jones)*

Below: Stranraer's magnificent **Caledonian Princess**. In this shot we can see to full advantage her attractive and, for a Channel railway steamer, unique, livery with buff colours extending to her deck houses. Above, the black-topped buff funnel carries the Caledonian red lion rampant. Aft, she proudly displays Stranraer as her port of registry, forever a curiosity in southern ports as she went on to become Sealink's most travelled steamer. *(Bruce Peter collection)*

Tragically, the new *Princess Victoria* met an untimely end, being lost on passage to Larne on 31st January 1953. The Court of Inquiry later declared that as the *Princess Victoria* was, to some degree experimental, it was all the more incumbent upon her owners to keep her design and construction under constant and expert review as experience was gained. Their failure to do so was a contribution to the disaster.

British Railways responded to Stranraer's needs by transferring the Dover train ferry *Hampton Ferry* to maintain a car ferry service during the summer of 1953. Car traffic continued to grow and the 'Hampton' went north again in 1954 and continued to do so each summer thereafter. The decision to order a replacement for the *Princess Victoria* was a long time coming and it was not until 5th April 1961 that renowned Dumbarton shipbuilder, Wm Denny & Bros, launched the splendid *Caledonian Princess*.

A measure of the doubts British Railways had in the route following the loss of the 'Victoria' can be seen in their segregation of the new ship from the rest of the fleet through the creation of the Caledonian Steam Packet (Irish Services) Ltd. Monitoring the isolated ship the implication was clear; if the service was not a success then the *Caledonian Princess* would be transferred elsewhere.

They need not have worried. In the ship's first year of operation passenger traffic increased by 20 per cent while vehicular traffic rose by 35 per cent. Into 1963 and beyond the figures continued their upward trend and two years later British Rail, who had taken over management of the route, ordered the *Antrim Princess*.

Pending delivery of the new ship British Rail chartered the Swedish-flag drive-through ferry *Stena Nordica* from Stena Line. Entering service from Larne on 14th February 1966 the ship was hugely popular, despite her small size, particularly with freight customers. In the event, the ship remained on the crossing beyond the arrival of the *Antrim Princess* until March 1971. Designed by the Danish consulting naval architects Knud E. Hansen A/S and built at Le Trait in France in 1965, the *Stena Nordica* was a drive-through vessel and her efficiently arranged vehicle deck and diesel propulsion were a revelation to the route's management. One unexpected advantage of chartering a Swedish ship was that, during the National Union of Seamen's strike later on in 1966, the *Stena Nordica* remained in service while the *Caledonian Princess* lay strike-bound at Stranraer. The *Stena Nordica* proved so satisfactory that she was kept on the Stranraer-Larne route for over five years.

In March 1966, an order was finally placed for a new Stranraer-Larne ferry with Hawthorn, Leslie (Shipbuilders) Ltd on Tyneside for the 3,730 gross ton *Antrim Princess*. As with the *Stena Nordica*, she was a drive-through diesel ferry and she was completed late in 1967. The *Stena Nordica* was however retained, meaning that a three-ship service was possible.

As for the *Antrim Princess*, she was notable being the company's first seagoing ship equipped with a bow door. She also broke with the long tradition of using steam turbine propulsion for its major ships, a move that introduced the funnel design that was to become synonymous with British Rail and Sealink. While the *Antrim Princess* was under construction, British Rail's London management seized direct control of

The sky may be blue and the seas calm, but some hardy passengers are dressed for the cold airs of the North Channel as the ***Caledonian Princess*** makes her way between Scotland and Northern Ireland. *(Bruce Peter collection)*

The interior of the 1967-built **Antrim Princess** was typical of her day with brightly lit and reflective deckheads designed to illuminate her enclosed public spaces. Tables were typically easy clean formica whilst the brightly coloured and high capacity banks of seating provided undercover shelter for her 1,200 passengers. BR's first drive-through ferry was a two-class ship, her First Class areas being at her forward end. In 1986 she became the Isle of Man Steam Packet Co's **Tynwald** until her sale to Italy four years later. *(Bruce Peter collection)*

Stranraer-Larne operations, which were very lucrative. BR's lawyers ascertained that, although the *Caledonian Princess* was CSP-owned, the right to operate the route was legally vested with the BR Board. As the CSP's Irish Services company deducted a proportion of revenue before passing on what was left to BR, the latter decided to take over operations and claim all profits. In the spring of 1966, while the *Caledonian Princess* was being overhauled at Greenock, the BR Board instructed contractors to remove the CSP lions rampant from her funnel and to repaint it in BR red with double-arrow logos. CSP management in Gourock was furious – but the symbolic change of the ship's identity signified that London was now in calling the shots. From the outset, the *Antrim Princess* was painted in the full BR livery.

At around the same time, thought was given to rebuilding the *Caledonian Princess* as a drive-through vessel, but this was deemed to be too complicated and, instead, a near-sister ship to the *Antrim Princess* was proposed. Much to the fury of British shipyard workers and the popular press, the lowest bid came from an Italian shipyard, Cantieri Navali Breda S.p.A., located in

an industrial suburb of Venice and a contract was signed in July 1969 with delivery scheduled for 1971. Named *Ailsa Princess*, the new vessel was notable for her stylish interiors and for a modified external livery treatment with white 'go faster' stripes around the funnel casing, devised by the Italians who pestered the BR naval architects Tony Rogan and Don Ripley to accept their ideas.

The *Caledonian Princess*, meanwhile, was shifted south, firstly to the Holyhead-Dun Laoghaire service, subsequently to the Fishguard-Rosslare route, then the Channel Islands services from Weymouth and Portsmouth and, finally, to serve as Dover's last steamer, on the Calais and Boulogne runs.

The freight ship *Darnia* was another Stena import and became something of a political hot potato in Labour Government circles at the time. The case was made that this foreign ship was not only badly needed at Stranraer but that being capable of double-deck loading of freight she was one of the few available that could navigate Loch Ryan at the time. In her original guise the ship could accommodate just 75 passengers but was later enlarged in a not entirely successful conversion to carry up to 412 passengers.

Shortly after the formation of Sealink UK Ltd and its subsidiary Sealink Scotland Ltd, a new ship was launched. The final railway new building for Scottish service was the 6,630 gross ton *Galloway Princess*, the first of four similar so-called 'Saint-class' ferries built by Harland & Wolff of Belfast, which was completed in 1980. Functional and robust, she was not only capacious, having space for 1,000 passengers and 309 cars, but gained a reputation as a solid performer in even the worst Irish Sea weather. Her arrival displaced the *Ailsa Princess* to deputise on southerly routes to Ireland and, most frequently, from Weymouth to Cherbourg. Upon privatisation, the Stranraer-Larne route was run by three regular ferries – the *Galloway Princess*, the *Darnia* and the *Antrim Princess*.

The 'Galloway' was an instant success and during her first four months in operation the company's market share on the North Channel rose by 8 per cent. The ship represented the very latest in car ferry design and went on to serve Stranraer impeccably until her withdrawal in 2002.

Going astern at Stranraer is the **Antrim Princess**. *(John Hendy collection)*

Above: The *Princess Maud* is seen arriving at Dun Laoghaire late in her career. Having no stabilisers, on a wild night she was said to be unbearable, her reputation for rolling mercilessly being well earned. While operating as a troop carrier during the war, she was extensively damaged at Dunkirk after a shell penetrated her engine room. She carried 1,360,870 troops during the war and on D Day she was anchored off the Normandy coast with 380 United States Army engineers and 20 tons of explosives and demolition charges. *(John Hendy collection)*

Left: Heysham's *Duke of York* was built in 1935 and is seen here outside a fleet mate in her original guise with two funnels. These were replaced by a single unit in 1950 when she was converted to oil burning and permanently transferred to the Eastern Region for service between Harwich and the Hook of Holland. *(Bruce Peter collection)*

Below: The new *Princess Victoria* entered service in 1947 and could carry 1,515 passengers, 40 cars and 70 tons of cargo. Lost on the last day of January 1953, the Court of Inquiry later declared that as she was to some extent an experimental ship it was all the more incumbent upon her owners to keep her design and construction under constant and expert review as experience in her operation was gained. Their failure to do so was a contribution to the disaster. *(Bruce Peter collection)*

Above: The First Class restaurant on board the *Cambria*. *(Bruce Peter collection)*

Top right: Sometimes things do go wrong. The *Hibernia* has just been launched at Belfast, straight into the opposite quay! Much smoke can be seen as tugs apply power to quickly recover the proceedings and bring the ship to the safety of the fit-out berth. *(Jim Ashby collection)*

Middle right: The *Cambria*'s First Class saloon. *(Bruce Peter collection)*

Right: The night owl at work. In the early hours of the morning the *Cambria* loads mail at Holyhead station. The ship is near the end of her career and would later be sold for service in the Red Sea. *(Captain George Davey collection)*

A new **Duke of Argyll** sweeps out of Heysham for Belfast in 1956. *(Bruce Peter collection)*

With the house flag of builders Harland & Wolff flying on her mainmast, the **Duke of Lancaster** is seen on sea trials along Belfast Lough. *(Jim Ashby collection)*

Above: The *Duke of Lancaster*'s entrance foyer. *(Jim Ashby collection)*

Below: Passengers board the *Duke of Lancaster* in May 1963. *(Jim Ashby collection)*

Below: The *Duke of Lancaster* , Boat Deck. *(Jim Ashby collection)*

Top: Berthed under the shadow of the old Station Hotel, the ***Cambria*** sits in the Departure Berth, No. 8, at Holyhead ready for her sailing to Dun Laoghaire at 03.15 the following morning. *(J.W. Sutherland/MLS Collection)*

Left: The ***Slieve Bawn*** on the 'Special Berth' at Holyhead, No. 9. *(A.G. Jones)*

Below: Holyhead heyday! From left to right are the ***Cambria*** awaiting her sailing to Dun Laoghaire, the ***Slieve Donard*** at the Goods Inward berth with the Harwich-based dredger ***Landguard*** sitting outside of her. Next is the cellular container ship ***Brian Boroime*** and finally the Dover Strait's ***Vortigern*** alongside the Refit Berth completing annual overhaul. *(J.W. Sutherland/MLS Collection)*

Above: Proudly displaying FR on her red funnel, the **St David** of the Fishguard & Rosslare Railways and Harbours Company. *(Bruce Peter collection)*

Left: A rare photo of the Waterford cargo ship **Great Western** in British Rail colours seen from the **St David** at Fishguard. *(David Heath)*

Bottom left: The **Stena Nordica** at Stranraer. Although considerably smaller than the **Caledonian Princess** she was hugely popular, particularly with freight customers. *(Jim Ashby collection)*

Bottom right: Seen from the bridge of the **Slieve Bearnagh** at Heysham during the 1966 seamen's strike is the cargo ship Selby. A single-screw ship, she and her sisters **Harrogate** and **Darlington** were not popular with Irish Sea masters. Ahead of the **Selby** is the **Duke of Argyll**. *(Jim Ashby collection)*

Above: A lovely view of the *Avalon* from the end of Dun Laoghaire's East Pier in August 1980. The ship is in her final month of service and on 8th September 1980 she left Dun Laoghaire on her final commercial sailing under the Sealink flag. Three months later, with funnel painted black and the first letter of her name removed, she arrived at Gadani Beach on 22nd January 1981. H.H. Steel Ltd commenced breaking immediately. *(Don Smith/Phototransport.com)*

Top right: Cars driving off the newly converted *Avalon* at Fishguard in 1975. *(British Rail)*

Middle right: The *Slieve Donard* at Holyhead's Goods Inward berth. At the weekend, on completion of cargo work, the ship would swing around to the Boathouse berth, astern of this view. This necessitated pinning the stern on to a king pile whilst a rope run across the dock pulled around the ship. This pile suffered so much damage by heavy use that the gang who maintained the piles named it the 'Golden Pile' for the amount of overtime it provided. *(J.W. Sutherland/MLS Collection)*

Right: Road, rail and sea with the *Stena Normandica* at Fishguard. *(Jim Ashby collection)*

Holyhead Ferry I

Above: Forward saloon on the *Holyhead Ferry I*. *(Bruce Peter collection)*

Left: Two berth cabin de luxe on the *Holyhead Ferry I*. *(Bruce Peter collection)*

Bottom left: Stairway on the *Holyhead Ferry I* *(Bruce Peter collection)*

Below: The bar on the *Holyhead Ferry I*. *(Bruce Peter collection)*

St Columba

Top: Arguably the finest ship built for the Holyhead routes was the *St Columba*. She was brought out from Aalborg in April 1977 by Senior Master Captain Len Evans and over a 19-year career on the route for which she was built endeared herself to millions of Irish Sea travellers. Effectively replacing three ships, the *St Columba* represented a much-needed boost for Holyhead which had been in decline for several years. By the end of her first year in service passenger carryings had increased by 27 per cent while freight had surged by 150 per cent. *(Adrian Herbert)*

Above left: The *St Columba*'s First Class lounge was dominated by this Franta Belsky mural depicting the journey of Colm Cille from Ireland to the Scottish island of Iona in 563AD. *(Bruce Peter collection)*

Above right: First Class side lounge. *(Bruce Peter collection)*

Left: : The *St Columba*'s rather more austere Second Class Lansdowne Road Bar. *(Bruce Peter collection)*

Left: The *Duke of Rothesay* resting at Holyhead between sailings during her final season in 1975 which was spent running to Dun Laoghaire. *(A.G. Jones)*

Left: Second Class lounge, *Duke of Rothesay*. *(Bruce Peter collection)*

Below left: The *Duke of Rothesay*'s First Class lounge. *((Bruce Peter collection)*

Below right: The *Stena Normandica* undergoing engine repairs at Holyhead in 1979. *(Ken Larwood)*

Top: Fisher's ***Brathay Fisher*** on charter at Holyhead in 1979. This single-screw container ship first saw service with British Rail at Holyhead in July and August 1971 before sailing to Harwich to cover dry-docking periods on the North Sea routes. She was back again on bareboat charter in 1974 and from November 1978 until October 1980. *(Ronnie Roberts collection)*

Above left: The ***Isle of Ely*** at Dublin. *(Jim Ashby collection)*

Above right: The ***Colchester***, otherwise known at Holyhead as the 'Long Slim Panatella'! *(John Hendy collection)*

Left: The former Stranraer ro-ro ***Ulidia*** laid up at Newhaven. *(John Hendy)*

Left: The *Darnia* swings off the berth at Stranraer. *(Ferry Publications Library)*

Below left: The Stranraer-based *Dalriada* leaves Holyhead for Dun Laoghaire in 1978. *(Bruce Peter collection)*

Bottom left: The *Stena Carrier* at Dover in July 1974 prior to taking up service at Stranraer as the *Ulidia*. The ship remained in operation with Sealink until the new *Galloway Princess* took up the run in 1980. *(A.G. Jones)*

Bottom right: The *Prinsessan Desirée*. *(Justin Merrigan)*

Left: Despite being a Dover ship, the **Anderida** was an Irish Sea regular, serving at Stranraer, Heysham and also at Holyhead. In May 1977 she was transferred to Fishguard, replacing the **Preseli** and is seen here at Rosslare in 1978. On 17th February 1979, while on passage from Rosslare to Fishguard, she suffered a serious engine room fire and was out of service for a month. On the arrival of the chartered **Stena Normandica**, the **Anderida** returned to Dover. *(John Hendy)*

Below: The **Galloway Princess** arriving at Larne. *(Ferry Publicatioins Library)*

Bottom left and right: The main passenger areas on board the **Galloway Princess**. *(Bruce Peter collection)*

Sealink
and before

CHAPTER SEVEN

Scotland

When the Second World War ended, it took a considerable time to return Scottish steamer services to normality. Vessels of the Clyde fleet were badly dilapidated – especially those requisitioned for military service, some of which were declared unfit for restoration and consigned for scrap. With a sharp upswing in passenger numbers, the LMS and LNER were hard-pressed to cope.

The LMS's Edwardian-era steamers *Duchess of Fife*, *King Edward* and *Duchess of Argyll* plus the LNER paddle steamer *Lucy Ashton* were all renovated and returned to service. Major reconstructions of the Craigendoran-based 1930s LNER vessels *Jeanie Deans* and *Talisman* were carried out and a new paddle steamer, the *Waverley*, was delivered in 1947 by A&J Inglis of Pointhouse to the LNER, initially to serve the Arrochar route but shortly switching to Rothesay and the Kyles of Bute. Though of handsome appearance, the *Waverley*'s design symbolised the deeply regressive mindset of her operator. Soon, exponential rises in the costs of fuel and staff wages greatly pressured the railway companies' managements. As the Clyde excursion fleet, in particular, carried a high proportion of working and lower-middle class day-trippers, significantly increasing fares was not an option if this clientele was to be retained.

The Transport Act of 1947 brought about a merger of the LMS and LNER Clyde steamer fleets under BTC control as part of the new British Railways. As the LMSR owned 50 per cent of shares in the Clyde and Hebridean steamer operator David MacBrayne, this too became a partially state-owned business upon the railway's nationalisation. On the East Coast, the BTC inherited car ferry services linking South and North Queensferry, adjacent to the Forth Railway Bridge. This crossing was operated by two mid-1930s built diesel-powered paddle ferries, the *Robert the Bruce* (the Clyde's first all-welded vessel) and the *Queen Margaret*. The BTC recognised early on that additional capacity would be needed and so in 1949 the *Mary Queen of Scots* was added followed in 1955 by the *Sir William Wallace*, which were also powered by paddles. The service was leased to shipbuilders, William Denny & Bros of Dumbarton who owned and operated the vessels although BR took a share of the profits.

In 1950, the entire Clyde fleet became one class, a belated recognition on the railway's part of the changing social order of the post-war era. Next, in February 1951, the BTC's Chairman, Lord Hurcomb, announced a £1 million modernisation of the fleet with four new diesel-powered passenger ferries to be built for rail-connected services to Dunoon, Rothesay and Millport plus three new car ferries for direct Gourock-Dunoon, Wemyss Bay-Rothesay and Fairlie (Ardrossan)-Brodick services. An eighth new building was to be a lake steamer for carrying tourists to view the 'bonny banks' of Loch Lomond, the CSP having taken over the loch's steamer service in 1952, plus the two charming if elderly vessels, *Princess May* and *Prince Edward*.

As most Clyde shipyards had full order books, two of the four passenger ferries were ordered from Messers Yarrow & Co. of Scotstoun, a builder more commonly associated with naval vessels and indeed the class did rather resemble minesweepers. The building of the remaining pair was subcontracted to A&J Inglis of Pointhouse, located upriver from Yarrows. Completed in 1953, the *Maid of Ashton*, *Maid of Argyll*, *Maid of Skelmorlie* and *Maid of Cumbrae* were compact and efficient, their British Polar diesel engines enabling speeds

Top left: The veteran paddle steamer *Duchess of Fife*, dating from 1903, was one of several elderly vessels inherited by British Railways upon its creation in 1947. The steamer is shown here on the Firth of Clyde in the early 1950s. *(A. Ernest Glen, Bruce Peter collection)*

Upper centre left: The *King Edward* of 1901 was a historically significant vessel, being the first ever commercial steam turbine ship. As with the *Duchess of Fife*, she continued to serve in the British Railways/Caledonian Steam Packet Company fleet until the early 1950s. Here, she is seen passing through the Kyles of Bute. *(A. Ernest Glen, Bruce Peter collection)*

Centre left: The splendid *Waverley*, shown here off Gourock Pier, was a post-war replacement for the steamer of the same name that had been lost at Dunkirk. The new vessel's design was, however, rather anachronistic. Built by A&J Inglis of Pointhouse for the LNER Arrochar route, she was soon switched to serve Rothesay and the Kyles of Bute instead. *(A. Ernest Glen, Bruce Peter collection)*

Bottom left: A stern-quarter view of the Craigendoran-based paddle steamer *Jeanie Deans*. Built by Fairfield Shipbuilding & Engineering Company of Govan and introduced in 1931, the vessel was extensively rebuilt after the Second World War. *(A. Ernest Glen, Bruce Peter collection)*

Top right: The turbine steamer *Duchess of Argyll* was another vessel of Edwardian vintage, having been delivered by William Denny & Bros to the Caledonian Steam Packet Company in 1906. She was withdrawn along with the *King Edward* at the end of the 1951 summer season. *(A. Ernest Glen, Bruce Peter collection)*

Above: A mid-1950s deck scene on the turbine steamer *Duchess of Hamilton*. In the era before overseas mass travel became possible, the Gourock-based steamer and her near-sister, the *Duchess of Montrose*, were popular with day-trippers and holiday-makers alike. Although the passenger accommodation on these 1920s-built ships was robustly outfitted, it was relatively spacious and, in fair weather, a pleasant short cruise could be enjoyed. *(A. Ernest Glen, Bruce Peter collection)*

The diesel-electric paddle steamer **Talisman**, dating from 1935, was inherited from the LNER and operated mainly from Craigendoran to Rothesay and the Kyles of Bute and from Wemyss Bay to Millport.. *(A. Ernest Glen, Bruce Peter collection)*

The turbine steamer **Queen Mary II** off Gourock in the early 1950s; the vessel's daily cruises from Glasgow to Tighnabruaich, via popular Clyde piers, were highly popular. *(A. Ernest Glen, Bruce Peter collection)*

The Forth car ferry **Queen Margaret** (built 1934) is seen approaching South Queensferry in the latter 1950s; the construction of a new road bridge in 1964 had rendered the 'Queensferry crossing' obsolete. *(A. Ernest Glen, Bruce Peter collection)*

In the early 1950s, the BTC commenced a much-needed new building programme to update the British Railways/Caledonian Steam Packet Company Clyde fleet. This involved the construction of four new passenger motor ships and three car ferries. Here, an example of the former type, the **Maid of Ashton** is seen in the Firth of Clyde in the mid-1950s. *(A. Ernest Glen, Bruce Peter collection)*

The turbine steamer **Duchess of Montrose** is seen off Gourock. *(A. Ernest Glen, Bruce Peter collection)*

During the winter, the excursion fleet was laid up in the Albert Harbour at Greenock, where in this mid-1950s view the paddle steamer **Jeanie Deans**, the cargo steamer **Kildonan** and the motor vessel **Countess of Breadalbane** are tied up together. The former was withdrawn at the end of the 1964 season. *(A. Ernest Glen, Bruce Peter collection)*

of over 15 knots to be achieved. Inboard, they somewhat resembled floating buses with rows of forward-facing fixed seating, but their large windows and effective heating made them relatively pleasant for short Clyde crossings.

Serving respectively Arran, Bute and Cowal, the new Clyde car ferries were given the names of these islands. The *Arran*, was ordered from William Denny & Bros of Dumbarton and delivered, her sisters, the *Bute* and the *Cowal*, being built by Ailsa of Troon and arriving in 1954. Twin-screw motor ships with their engines forward and vehicle access two-thirds aft, as well as carrying cars and some commercial vehicles, they also transported livestock and some general cargo. To cope with varying tides, an electric lift was fitted between the side ramps, using the same technology as on Royal Navy aircraft carriers to raise planes from the hanger to the flight deck. Each ferry could carry 650 passengers, the majority in a deckhouse forward of the vehicle ramp, containing a lounge with rows of fixed benches and a tea bar with space for 38. From the outset, they were a great success.

The investment in new tonnage allowed the oldest steamers to be withdrawn, the *King Edward* and *Duchess of Argyll* being the first to go after the 1951 summer season. The paddle steamer *Duchess of Fife* and the turbine *Glen Sannox* followed them to the breakers in 1953. That same year, the new Loch Lomond steamer *Maid of the Loch* was assembled and launched at Balloch from a kit of parts supplied by the builder of the *Waverley* and two of the 'Maids', A&J Inglis. Intended to replace a much smaller steamer, the *Princess May*, from the outset, the *Maid of the Loch* proved to be something of a 'white elephant'.

British Railways' Scottish shipping services included the operation of pleasure steamers on Loch Lomond, where the ***Prince Edward*** – a vessel dating from 1911 – continued to operate in the mid-1950s. *(A. Ernest Glen, Bruce Peter collection)*

As car ownership continued rapidly to increase, it became clear that a fourth, considerably larger ferry would be needed for the Arran route. In 1955, an order was placed with the Ailsa Shipbuilding Co. of Troon for the *Glen Sannox*, with a capacity of 1,100 passengers, 40 cars and general cargo.

The introduction of the new Clyde ferry fleet preceded a gradual loosening of centralised control from the BTC in London to its various subsidiaries. In parallel, the Caledonian Steam Packet Company's 'lion rampant' pennant appeared again on mastheads instead of British Railways' house flag.

So far as Clyde services were concerned, passenger

The northern outpost of the British Railways/Caledonian Steam Packet Company's operations was the short ferry route from Kyle of Lochalsh to the Isle of Skye. Here, the turntable ferry ***Kyleakin*** is seen at Kyle of Lochalsh in the early 1960s. Turntable ferries' vehicle decks could pivot round, enabling them to load and offload on piers parallel with the hull. In the mid-20th century, the type was commonplace in the West Highlands. *(A. Ernest Glen, Bruce Peter collection)*

Top: The paddle steamer *Jupiter* reverses away from Greenock in the early 1960s. The mid-1930s Fairfield-built vessel operated mainly on short ferry-like crossings of the Firth of Clyde but could carry only a few cars amidships, loaded over the paddle boxes. With road vehicle ownership rising exponentially in the 1950s, a new approach was urgently needed. *(A. Ernest Glen, Bruce Peter collection)*

Above left: Three new car ferries – the *Arran*, *Bute* and *Cowal* – were built to serve on the Ardrossan/Fairlie-Brodick, Wemyss Bay-Rothesay and Gourock-Dunoon routes respectively. As well as cars and some commercial vehicles, they also transported livestock and some general cargo, for which purpose derricks were installed at the stern. To cope with varying tides, an electric lift was fitted between the side ramps. Here the *Bute* is seen in Rothesay Bay in the mid-1950s. *(A. Ernest Glen, Bruce Peter collection)*

Above right: Another winter view of the Albert Harbour with the *Jupiter* berthed nearest to the camera and the *Marchioness of Graham*, *Duchess of Hamilton* and *Duchess of Montrose* in the background. *(A. Ernest Glen, Bruce Peter collection)*

Left: A new Loch Lomond steamer, the *Maid of the Loch*, was introduced in 1953 but soon proved rather over-dimensioned for such custom as was by then available. After years of disuse, the vessel is currently undergoing restoration. *(A. Ernest Glen, Bruce Peter collection)*

Top: In the early 1960s, the Clyde excursion fleet's decline was accelerating thanks to rising operational costs, ageing vessels and a decline in custom. The newest of the major units was the paddle steamer ***Waverley***, seen here in the Firth of Clyde in the early 1960s. *(A. Ernest Glen, Bruce Peter collection)*

Above left: The ***Queen Mary II*** leaves Bridge Wharf in Glasgow at the commencement of a Clyde excursion in the early 1960s; in the mid-50s, the vessel was re-boilered and fitted with a single, wider funnel and this work enabled her to serve for over two further decades. *(A. Ernest Glen, Bruce Peter collection)*

Above right: The small motor vessel ***Countess of Breadalbane*** is seen in the Firth of Clyde. Built in the mid-1930s by William Denny & Bros for service on Loch Awe, in 1952, her superstructure was dismantled, enabling her hull to be carried by road to Loch Fyne. After rebuilding at Denny's yard, she entered Clyde service. *(A. Ernest Glen, Bruce Peter collection)*

Left: The BTC under-estimated the growth of car ownership and so its initial Clyde car ferries soon were operating at capacity. The solution was to build an additional, significantly larger ferry for the Arran run, the ***Glen Sannox***, which entered service in 1957. Here, she is seen at Brodick Pier early in her career. *(A. Ernest Glen, Bruce Peter collection)*

Top: The Gourock-Dunoon ferry *Cowal* is seen crossing the Clyde in the latter 1950s. (*A. Ernest Glen, Bruce Peter collection*)

Above left: In 1965, once British Railways had been rebranded as 'British Rail', the remaining units of the Clyde steamer and ferry fleets were repainted with monastral blue hulls, but retained their Caledonian Steam Packet buff yellow funnels, which were adorned with lions rampant, rather than British Rail's corporate 'double arrow' logo. Here, the blue-hulled *Queen Mary II* is seen leaving Greenock in 1965. That year, there were only four traditional excursion steamers in service – the *Caledonia* and *Waverley* stationed at Craigendoran, the *Duchess of Hamilton* at Gourock and the *Queen Mary II* in Glasgow. (*A. Ernest Glen, Bruce Peter collection*)

Above right: The ferry *Glen Sannox* is seen in the Firth of Clyde shortly after repainting in the new British Rail hull livery. (*A. Ernest Glen, Bruce Peter collection*)

Left: The repainted *Duchess of Hamilton* at Gourock. *A. Ernest Glen, Bruce Peter collection*

The **Waverley** approaches Gourock in her new British Rail/CSP livery. *(A. Ernest Glen, Bruce Peter collection)*

numbers slid from 4,367,173 in 1959 to 3,582,303 in 1963 – and it was the excursion steamers, not the car ferries, that were solely responsible for this reduction. With the exception of the *Waverley*, those that remained were ageing and costly to keep running. Labour relations also declined with regular strikes over pay and conditions and less attention given to vessels' upkeep. Thus, just as the travelling public's expectations were increasing, the level of service provision on CSP vessels was lowered. At this point, the *Jeanie Deans* and the *Duchess of Montrose* – the oldest of the remaining steamers – were withdrawn and, by 1965, there were only four steamers left on the Clyde – the *Caledonia* and *Waverley* stationed at Craigendoran, the *Duchess of Hamilton* at Gourock and the *Queen Mary II* in Glasgow. That year, the new British Rail blue hull livery was applied to the CSP fleet. As the CSP's directors were not enamoured with BR's red funnel with 'double arrow' – which would make their ships less easily distinguishable from those of MacBraynes – they insisted on retaining the existing buff yellow. The need for a corporate logo was resolved by applying red lions rampant – not the modern image British Rail's

London management had in mind, but at least with a distinct local character.

On Scotland's East Coast, meanwhile, a new Forth Road Bridge was completed in 1964, rendering the historic Queensferry crossing obsolete. Its newest vessel, the *Sir William Wallace* had entered service only in 1956, but now she was withdrawn along with her three elder sisters, which were consigned for scrapping; the *Sir William Wallace* was sold to a Belgian owner but survived only until 1970.

The need for a 'joined-up' transport policy, alongside major cost-cutting, were among the factors which prompted a radical reorganisation of Scottish West Coast shipping services. In 1970, the CSP and its Clyde operations were handed over to a new Edinburgh-headquartered state transport authority, the Scottish Transport Group (STG). Shipping services of the CSP and David MacBrayne were thus integrated with those of the Scottish Bus Group – a sure sign that road had overtaken rail as Scotland's dominant mode of transport.

The **Duchess of Hamilton** is seen at Gourock Pier. *(A. Ernest Glen, Bruce Peter collection)*

The paddle steamer **Caledonia** was one of only two to remain in service in the British Rail era. *(A. Ernest Glen, Bruce Peter collection)*

Sealink
and before

CHAPTER EIGHT

Estuarine and
Lake Services

RIVER DART: DARTMOUTH-KINGSWEAR FERRY

Railway involvement in the Kingswear to Dartmouth ferry service stretched back to 1864 when the Dartmouth & Torbay Railway opened its line to Kingswear, leasing the ferry rights to its associate concern the Dartmouth Steam Packet Company. New pontoons were built on both sides of the Dart estuary and a new station was constructed on the west side of the river at Dartmouth. From here passengers could purchase tickets for trains at either Kingswear or up river at Totnes.

The Great Western Railway (GWR) took over the running of trains on the Dartmouth & Torbay Railway in 1876 at which time they acquired a 25-year lease for the operation of the Dart ferry service. Two years later the GWR also acquired ownership of the Dartmouth & Torbay Railway.

The GWR's only new vessel for the Kingswear – Dartmouth ferry service was the Falmouth-built *The Mew* in 1908. Named after a well-known local sea-mark, the twin-screw vessel could accommodate 547 passengers but following the Great War, her after deckhouse was removed to allow the carriage of up to five motor cars.

Shortly after nationalisation and now under the ownership of British Railways (Western Region), further modifications were made to the ageing ship and, in an effort to make her look more modern, her tall stovepipe funnel was replaced by a wider, shorter, elliptical version. With efforts to keep the steamer operational becoming increasingly more challenging, she was finally withdrawn from service in October 1954.

During *The Mew's* refit periods, it was the practise to charter the River Dart Steamboat Company's paddle steamer *Totnes Castle* to maintain the ferry service and following her withdrawal from service, a further charter period ensued. However, it was then decided to charter the Millbrook Steamboat & Trading Co's motor vessel *Lady Elizabeth* which proved rather more economical to operate. Other diesel vessel charters followed until in 1956, BR ordered two small, 150-passenger, vessels from Blackmore & Sons of Bideford. At a ceremony at Kingswear in March 1957 they were named after the famous Elizabethan seamen *Adrian Gilbert* and *Humphrey Gilbert*.

In 1972, following the closure of the railway line to Kinsgwear, British Rail also sold the vessels and the Dart ferry service to Dartmouth Borough Council and in 1976 they were again sold for use on the St Mawes ferry on the River Fal. As we shall see, both vessels were later repurchased by BR for intended service on the Thames.

PLYMOUTH: TENDERING TO OCEAN LINERS

The GWR commenced a tender service to ocean liners calling at Plymouth in 1873. When not in use as tenders, a series of seasonal coastal excursions was normally operated.

Three vessels passed into the hands of British Railways in 1948. The *Sir Francis Drake* was built by Cammell Laird at Birkenhead in 1908 and lasted in service until 1953. Interestingly, although her sister ship *Sir Walter Raleigh* was not seen as worthy of restoration after the war and was sold for breaking in 1947, she was quickly resold and became a tender at Cherbourg where as the *Ingenieur Reibell* she survived until 1968.

The *Sir John Hawkins* was built by Earle's at Hull in 1929 but was withdrawn from service in 1961 following the French Line's decision to stop calling at Plymouth. The final vessel was

Top left: Seen alongside at Kingswear in March 1957 are the sister vessels **Adrian Gilbert** and **Humphrey Gilbert** which maintained the ferry service until sold to the Dartmouth Council in 1972. They were later repurchased for use on the Tilbury ferry. *(John Hendy collection)*

Top right: **The Mew** of 1908 served the Dartmouth-Kingswear passage until 1954, latterly also being able to accommodate up to five cars on her after deck. *(Jim Ashby collection)*

Above left: The tender **Sir Richard Grenville** was introduced in 1931 to cater for the considerable amount of liner traffic then calling at Plymouth. Withdrawn from service after this had all but ceased in 1963, she served the final six years of her career running between Jersey and St Malo. *(John Hendy collection)*

Above right: The **Catherine** (of 1903) was one of a quartet of steamers built for the Tilbury-Gravesend ferry in the years before the First World War. Along with her sisters **Rose** and **Edith** (the **Gertrude** was sold in 1932) they maintained the route until in 1960 they received the suffix 'II' in readiness for their diesel replacements. This image dates from May 1954. *(Justin Merrigan collection)*

Below: The car ferry **Tessa** alongside at West Street in Gravesend in October 1959. Having been built in 1924, the coal-fired vessel could carry about 25 cars and 250 passengers. Both she and the slightly larger **Mimie** continued to trade after the Dartford Tunnel opened but they were finally withdrawn at the end of 1964. *(Justin Merrigan collection)*

Seen in January 1961, the second **Catherine** was one of the trio of ships built in Southampton in 1960/61 to serve as replacements for their elderly coal burning predecessors. With the route losing money, the **Rose** was sold to Scotland in 1967 while the **Catherine** was laid aside in 1981 leaving the **Edith** to operate the service alone. *(Justin Merrigan collection)*

the *Sir Richard Grenville* which was also product of Earle's in 1931. With declining numbers of liner calls, she was eventually withdrawn in 1963 after which she was sold and then resold again to Jersey Lines who named her *La Duchesse de Normandie*. Her new service linked Jersey and St Malo, reviving the route of the Southern Railway's *Brittany* and space was created to carry up to 25 cars and 550 passengers.

The success of the new ship and service prompted Jersey Line to purchase the fuel thirsty Newhaven vessel *Brighton* in 1966. Renamed *La Duchesse de Bretagne* the ship was engaged on a series of complex and demanding sailings from Torquay and Weymouth to St Malo and the Channel Islands. The line folded in 1969 after which both their ships were sold for breaking.

RIVER THAMES: TILBURY – GRAVESEND FERRY

In 1948, British Railways (Eastern Region) inherited five steam driven vessels from the London Midland & Scottish Railway (LMS).

Built for the London Tilbury & Southend Railway in 1901, 1903 and 1911 respectively, the passenger ferries *Rose*, *Catherine* and *Edith* were products of the AW Robertson yard of Canning Town in London. A fourth vessel was the *Gertrude* (1901) which was sold to the New Medway Steam Packet Company in 1932 and renamed *Rochester Queen* for the Strood – Southend service. A year later she was acquired by Bland of Gibraltar for use as a tender and, *named Gibel Derif*, was broken up in 1962.

The other three ferries received the suffix 'II' to their names in 1960 in readiness for their replacements. They were very basic and Spartan little ships and retained oil lighting until the end of their days. The *Catherine II* was the first to go and the end of 1960 and it was left to her sisters to maintain the service until the close of February the following year.

The car ferry service between Tilbury and Gravesend was maintained by the *Tessa* and *Mimie*. Ordered by the LMS, the *Tessa* was built in 1924 by Lytham Shipbuilding & Engineering co while the *Minmie* was a product of Ferguson's Port Glasgow yard three years later. Side loading arrangements allowed between 20 and 30 cars with 250 passengers (*Tessa*)/ 300 passengers (*Mimie*) to be carried. On the Tilbury side, both car and passenger ferries used the same pontoon whereas at Gravesend, the car ferries operated from West Street and the

passenger ships from slightly downstream at the Town Pier.

When in November 1963 the first Dartford Tunnel was opened, the days of the Tilbury – Gravesend car ferry were numbered and although BR attempted to maintain their rival service, trade suffered and the service was eventually closed on the final day of 1964.

Replacements for the three steam driven passenger ferries came in the form of three vessels of the same names which were built by White's at Southampton in 1960 (*Catherine* and *Edith*) and 1961 (*Rose*). With capacity for as many as 475 passengers, speedy embarkation was via hydraulically operated gangways on both sides. Up river cruising became a popular summer pastime with the *Edith* being fitted with a PA system and basic catering facilities.

With the decline of shipping and therefore of workers using Tilbury Docks, the *Rose* soon became surplus to requirements and in 1967 she was taken by the Caledonian Steam Packet Co for use on the Largs – Millport (Great Cumbrae) service for which she was renamed *Keppel*.

The route continued to lose money with the number of passengers using the link dropping from three million to less than one million. Subsidies from local councils assisted BR in their efforts to keep the service profitable but when in 1976, they were withdrawn, BR applied to rid themselves of the ailing route. After this had been refused by Parliament, in an effort to replace the *Catherine* and *Edith* and make considerable cost savings, the former Kingswear – Dartmouth passenger ferries *Adrian Gilbert* and *Humphrey Gilbert* were once more taken into nationalised ownership. The vessels were re-engined and significantly upgraded only to be refused passenger certificates to operate the link due to their low freeboard and minimal passenger carrying capability. Red faces were the order of the day as the two vessels were again offered for sale while the *Catherine* and *Edith* were forced to carry on as usual. In readiness for privatisation, their ownership passed to Sealink UK Ltd in 1979 but the *Catherine* was laid up in 1981 and cannibalised in order to keep her sister operational. She was eventually sold for excursion work on the River Tyne in 1989.

After the Stena Line takeover of Sealink British Ferries in 1991, the route was eventually sold to White Horse Ferries who chartered the *Edith* until their own vessel entered service in the following year. She was subsequently sold for conversion to a houseboat. In 2000, the ownership of the route passed to the Lower Thames & Medway Passenger Boat Co who presently operate the link with the former Portsmouth - Gosport ferry, the 124 passenger *Duchess M* (ex *Vesta*).

HUMBER: NEW HOLLAND – HULL FERRY

At the time of nationalisation in 1948, The London & North Eastern Railway's (LNER) three Humber paddle steamers became part of the British Railways (Eastern Region) fleet. This lasted until in 1959 their management was transferred to Associated Humber Line (AHL) and the ships adopted a broad red band on their buff, black topped funnels. In 1965, they were repainted again, in the colours of British Rail but continued to be managed by AHL.

The coal-fired ships in question were firstly the sisters *Tattershall Castle* and *Wingfield Castle* which were built by William Grey & Co at West Hartlepool in 1934. With capacity of about 20 cars and up to 1,200 passengers, in addition to their ferry duties they were also involved in excursions out to Spurn Head at the mouth of the Humber and also to Grimsby. The A&J Inglis-built *Lincoln Castle* joined the fleet in August 1941,

Top: Approaching the Essex bank of the Thames on board one of the car ferries, the new diesel passenger vessel *Catherine* lies alongside the Tilbury Landing Stage. *(John Hendy collection)*

Above left and right: The sisters *Wingfield Castle* and *Tattershall Castle* entered service in 1934 and could carry about 20 cars on their after decks along with as many as 1,200 passengers. They were withdrawn in 1972/74 when the *Farringford* came north to replace them until the bridge finally opened in June 1981. The 'Wingfield' has been preserved at her birthplace at West Hartlepool while a greatly modified 'Tattershall' is today a floating pub on the Thames. *(Both Bruce Peter collection)*

Left: The Clyde-built *Lincoln Castle* joined the route in 1940 but was prematurely withdrawn with serious boiler problems in March 1978 leaving the *Farringford* to maintain the service until its demise. *(J.W. Sutherland/MLS collection)*

The *Brightlingsea* of 1925 maintained the Harwich-Felixstowe ferry until sold by BR in 1961. The vessel was then purchased by private ownership and continued to operate the link until 1992. *(John Hendy)*

presenting an altogether more modern appearance with a proper mainmast and her funnel and boilers both forward of her paddle boxes. Like her operating partners she was also used on excursions, carrying almost 100 more passengers when involved in these duties.

Plans for a new ferry were mooted during 1968 but the threat of a fixed link across the Humber was to cast its shadow across the service for the remainder of its existence.

The *Tattershall Castle* was the first of the trio to be withdrawn in September 1972 and was later sold for static use on the River Thames where, in a greatly disfigured condition, she still lies. She was followed in March 1974 by the *Wingfield Castle* which was replaced in service by the surplus Isle of Wight car ferry *Farringford*. Her folding bow and stern doors were duly replaced by a flat, punt-like, bow and stern and for the remainder of her career she became a side loader, cars in preference being loaded towards the stern section in order to prevent them from being covered in spray during passage. As for the 'Wingfield' she very much enjoyed a peripatetic post Sealink career until in 1985 she was brought back to her birthplace where she became a museum ship.

During her annual refit in March 1978, it was discovered that the *Lincoln Castle* required a new boiler which would take nine months to build at a cost of £150,000. With the imminent opening of the Humber Bridge, the vessel was immediately withdrawn from service leaving the *Farringford* to soldier on alone. During her refit periods in 1979 and again in 1980, the *Farringford's* former running partner on the Lyimington – Yarmouth route, the *Freshwater*, deputised at Hull while damage to the *Farringford* in October 1979 saw the Bridlington excursion vessel *Yorkshire Belle* hastily brought in and again during the following February.

With the Humber Bridge finally opening for traffic in June 1981, the 178 years of the Humber ferry came to an end and after a sale to Western Ferries, the *Farringford* was broken up locally in March 1984.

RIVER STOUR: HARWICH – FELIXSTOWE FERRY

Inherited from the LNER, the Eastern Region of British Railways took over the operation of the Harwich (Essex) – Felixstowe (Suffolk) ferry in 1948. The service was operated by four small motor launches: the *Pinmiill* of 1910 which was purchased in 1912 by the Great Eastern Railway, the *Epping* and *Hainault* of 1914 which were both built for the Great Eastern and the rather larger *Brightlingsea* of 1925, the first

vessel built for the LNER. Her arrival appears to have relegated the *Pinmill* to mainly work boat duties after which time she appears to have only seen spasmodic ferry service. The service to Shotley, on the north bank of the Stour, was not restarted after the war.

Plans to close the Felixstowe link were announced in 1959 but a public outcry brought a two-year reprieve. However, on New Year's Eve 1961 the service was duly terminated but under the wing of the newly formed Orwell & Harwich Navigation Co it was restarted using the *Brightlingsea* on 1st May 1962. The service was taken over by the Felixstowe Dock and Railway Co (owned by the European Ferries Group) in 1979 and sold again six years later. It continued until 1992 when, due to port expansion, the vessel was denied access to Feliixstowe Dock.

On the closure of the BR service in 1961, the 1914 pair of vessels were sold off for private use while the *Pinmill* was retained by BR for use as a work boat at Parkeston Quay, ferrying crews out to their vessels on the buoys in the River Stour. This work appears to have continued until 1987 when she was laid up after sinking.

LAKE WINDERMERE

The four large passenger vessels which sailed on England's largest lake all boasted an historic railway ancestry. The oldest was the Furness Railway's canoe-bowed *Tern* of 1891. She was built by Forrest & Sons at Wyvenhoe in Essex while their Clyde-built *Swift* dated from 1900. The two largest and most modern vessels were the double-decked *Teal* and *Swan* which were built by Vickers Armstrong at Barrow for the LMS in 1936 and 1938.

Services operated from Easter and then from May to October, the vessels operating from their Lakeside rail connected base at the lake's southern end and sailing to Bowness and Ambleside in the north.

The *Swift* was laid aside in 1982 (and eventually broken up in 1996) but the same year saw Sealink take over the operation of Coniston Water's former Furness Railway's vessel *Gondola* (1859) before the National Trust succeeded them in the following year.

Following the acquisition of Sealink UK Ltd by Sea Containers, in 1984 the Windermere services were transferred to the ownership of their Hotels & Leisure Division, SeaCo Inc. who until 1993 traded as the Windermere Iron Steamboat Company. The operation was then sold to the ownership of Windermere Lake Cruises.

Left: At the wheel of the Windermere excursion vessel *Teal* in July 1979 are Philip Ridley and John Marrow. *(Jim Ashby)*

Middle left: The *Swan* was built at Barrow for the London Midland & Scottish Railway (LMS) in 1938. *(Jim Ashby)*

Below: The Barrow-built *Teal* was added to the service by the LMS in 1936. *(Jim Ashby)*

Bottom view: The *Tern* entered service in 1891, her canoe-shaped bow being very much a feature of her construction. Following her conversion to diesel propulsion she was provided with a rather unsympathetic stump funnel but under private ownership a more appropriate stove pipe funnel has been fitted. *(Jim Ashby)*

*Associated
Companies*

MANX LINE

Upon the opening of the port of Heysham by the railway in 1904, regular passenger services commenced to Belfast and during the summer months to the Isle of Man.

With the grouping in 1923 of the smaller railways companies into the 'big four', the newly formed LMS took charge of the operations of the Lancashire & Yorkshire Railway, the London & North Western Railway and the Midland Railway. In 1920 the latter's *Manxman* was sold to the Isle of Man Steam Packet Company who went on to run the service to Douglas until the outbreak of World War II when the *Victoria* returned light to Douglas after the cancellation of her sailing from Heysham on 4th September 1939. It was not until 1953 that a scheduled sailing operated between Douglas and Heysham, taken by the Steam Packet's handsome *Mona's Isle* of 1951. Between 1953 and 1974 a link was maintained with the Isle of Man, but only during the summer months and even then with just a handful of sailings a week.

And that was that, until 1977 when the Isle of Man Government announced plans to provide facilities at Douglas to service a new floating linkspan to be owned and installed by a Manx company for a new daily passenger ro-ro service to Heysham. Ro-ro services had long been running throughout the British Isles and were widely accepted as the cost effective way of achieving fast delivery of freight; widely accepted except on the Isle of Man where for several years there was ongoing debate over the possible introduction of such a service.

The Isle of Man Steam Packet Company was infuriated at the suggestion of a new service by a new Manx company. At that time the Manx Government was the single largest shareholder in the Steam Packet and the latter, with its fleet of side-loading car ferries, was vehemently opposed to the notion of a ro-ro operation for the Island, despite it being actively pursued by the Isle of Man Harbour Board.

The new Manx Line operation was launched late in the season on 26th August 1978 using the former Spanish ferry *Monte Castillo*. The cause of the delay was a refit dogged with shipyard troubles and in fact the ferry only left the dock after Manx Line's marine superintendent Captain Andrew Douglas threatened to lay waste to the town of Leith, just as his ancestors of the 'Black Douglas' clan had done centuries before!

The ship arrived at Douglas for the first time eight months earlier for berthing trials. As the *Manx Viking* the new ship would have a seismic influence on not only transportation methods for the Island but also on the very future of the Isle of Man Steam Packet Company; but not before itself first sailing perilously close to the brink of oblivion.

Numerous breakdowns with the ship all conspired against the new operation which was headed by six times world motorcycle champion and five times winner of the Manx TT Geoff Duke OBE with Board members from the independent Manx shipping company Ronagency. But it was perhaps an indication of how entrenched the Steam Packet was in its time-honoured way of doing business that Manx Line continued to trade until November 1978 when it was rescued from financial ruin by British Rail who took a 60 per cent shareholding, the remaining 40 per cent being taken by James Fisher & Sons of Barrow.

Within a matter of days of the formation of Sealink (IOM) disaster struck. On 1st December the company's new linkspan was severely damaged during an easterly storm. At its height

Top: The *Manx Viking* was the first ro-ro ferry to service the Isle of Man and is seen here looking resplendent in her original blue and white Manx Line livery. *(Don Smith/Phototransport.com)*

Above: Stern in at Douglas in Sealink livery the *Manx Viking* differed from other Sealink ships in carrying a gold-coloured sculpted "three legs of man" on her funnels rather than the standard BR double arrow logo. *(Ken Larwood)*

Left: The *Bolton Abbey* and her sister ship *Melrose Abbey* (II) were built to replace elderly tonnage on the Hull – Rotterdam route and entered since in 1958/59. Both were lengthened by 52 ft in 1967/68. *(Bruce Peter collection)*

Built at Hull for the Hull & Netherlands Steamship Co, the stately *Melrose Abbey* was added to the Hull-Rotterdam link in 1929 carrying 120 passengers in two classes. In 1935 she came under the management of the AHL. Early in 1959 she was replaced by a motor vessel of the same name and was sold to Greece for inter-island cruising. *(Paul Clegg/John Hendy collection)*

the structure broke free of its shoreside connection and partially capsized. In order to maintain a presence and to honour its commitments to freight customers the company resorted to offering a lo-lo service with the chartered coasters *Eden Fisher* and *Poole Fisher*. It was not until the following May that the *Manx Viking* was back on the run using a temporary linkspan installed on the north side of the Edward Pier until its own ramp was back in full operation in July. A much needed extension to the breakwater at Douglas was completed in 1983.

With the might of Britain's largest ferry company behind it Manx Line's operation was soon taking a large share of market proportion from the Steam Packet. From time to time engine trouble disrupted the *Manx Viking*'s sailings but in such cases Sealink always provided a relief vessel which only further served to cast an unwelcome spotlight on the competition's operation.

Eventually the Isle of Man Steam Packet took the plunge and introduced its first ro-ro ship, the *Mona's Isle* in October 1984. It was however too little, too late and after a disastrous first season the recently acquired ship was quickly sold off. By now the Steam Packet was in dire financial straits and in very real danger of closure. The only option available to the historic company was a merger with the recently privatised Sealink,

brokered by Sea Containers. It is fair to say that supporters of Sealink were most frustrated with their new owners; it would have been quite simple for Sea Containers to allow the Isle of Man Steam Packet to succumb to its self-inflicted wounds and allow Sealink to pick up the pieces. Instead on 1st April 1985 it took a 40 per cent shareholding and placed four members on the Steam Packet Board.

Following the rather unhappy marriage, the *Manx Viking* returned to Douglas from annual overhaul in Steam Packet colours hastily daubed over her Sealink colours. In a display of defiance her crew continued to fly the Sealink house flag at the mast but the Steam Packet was determined to erase any trace of the pioneering company. At the end of September 1986 the *Manx Viking* quietly slipped out of Douglas for the last time. In true Viking style the ship's Irish Sea career was anything but sedentary but her place in history as the provider of the first full-time ro-ro service to the Isle of Man is assured.

Full control of the Steam Packet was eventually taken by Sea Containers in 1996 and in 1998 they introduced the *Ben-my-Chree*, the first new build ship for the company since the *Lady of Mann* in 1976. Five years later Sea Containers sold the Isle of Man Steam Packet for £142 million.

Entering service in 1956/57 were the *Kirkham Abbey* and *Byland Abbey* which were built for the North Eastern Region of the BTC for service from Goole to Copenhagen. They were both managed by the AHL but were sold to Ellerman's Wilson Line in 1965 for whom they were renamed *Ariosto* and *Angelo*. *(Justin Merrigan collection)*

ASSOCIATED HUMBER LINES

One of the concerns passing to the new British Transport Commission (BTC) in 1948 was the Associated Humber Steamship Lines Control Committee (AHL). This was a managing company formed in 1935 to oversee a rather complex service network involving no fewer than 30 ships operating between the Humber ports of Goole, Grimsby and Hull to Rotterdam, Amsterdam, Antwerp, Ghent, Dunkirk, Hamburg and Copenhagen.

The AHL took over the operation, but not the ownership, of ships and services then owned by both the competing LMS at Goole (via their subsidiary the Goole Steam Shipping Co.) and the LNER's Great Central section at Grimsby. In addition, the Hull-based Hull & Netherlands Steamship Co. Ltd was a subsidiary of the LNER while the railway company also enjoyed a controlling interest in the Wilson's & North Eastern Railway Shipping Co. Ltd.

At nationalisation in January 1948, the Goole fleet came under the wing of the London Midland Region until it was transferred to the North Eastern Region during the early 1950s. The two companies at Hull, although controlled by the BTC, continued to operate under AHL management but services from Grimsby were not revived after the war.

In 1948 the Goole fleet consisted of nine elderly cargo steamers, the oldest being the *Irwell* of 1906 and the newest the *Aire* of 1931. They were all named after rivers in Lancashire and Yorkshire as before the grouping of 1923, the ships and services were operated by the Lancashire & Yorkshire Railway. The Hull fleet was four strong and ranged in age from the *Bury* of 1910 to the *Melrose Abbey* of 1929.

However, in February 1957 Associated Humber Lines Ltd was registered and took over the ownership of the combined Humber operation with the BTC now owning a 91 per cent share and Ellerman's Wilson Line the remainder. Thus, the majority of the existing fleet was transferred to the new entity and the fleet renewal programme, involving no fewer than 12 vessels, was continued. Excluded from AHL ownership were two new Goole-Copenhagen diesel vessels (*Kirkham Abbey* and *Byland Abbey*) which continued to be 'railway' ships under AHL management until their sale in 1965 to Ellerman's Wilson Line. At the time of the AHL's formation as a ship-owning company, the Hull & Netherlands Steamship Co. and Wilson's & North Eastern Railway Steamship Co. were wound up.

The late 1950s had seen the withdrawal of the old pre-war steamers, all of which had carried a handful of passengers although the Rotterdam vessels *Bury* and *Melrose Abbey* had passenger certificates for over 100. Their replacements came in the form of diesel-driven cargo-only ships but unfortunately they were introduced at a time when the containerisation of cargoes was growing and it is noteworthy that in 1959 the *Container Enterprise* and the *Container Venturer* entered service at Heysham; the first railway ship specially designed for carrying containers. On the North Sea the AHL failed to move with the times and chose to build ships involving the time-consuming loading and unloading of general cargo and which would eventually lead to their demise.

Control of AHL was transferred to the new Transport Holding Company (THC) in January 1963. The THC was directly responsible to the Ministry of Transport and under their management a significant consolidation of services began. A joint venture was launched with Germany's Argo Line in 1963, with a passenger-cargo link between Hull/Goole-Bremen and

A lorry reverses onto the **Bardic Ferry** at Tilbury. No health and safety high viz requirements in those days! *(Bruce Peter collection)*

The offices of ASN at 25 Whitehall, London SW1. *(Ferry Publications Library)*

Hamburg, the *Whitby Abbey* sailing alongside Argo's *Adler* and *Mowe*. Sadly the passenger operation on the route was a short-lived affair and in September 1966 the *Whitby Abbey* was replaced by the *Darlington*.

The service from Goole to Rotterdam was closed in August 1964 and AHL's third ship contribution was also removed from the Copenhagen service. As a result, the *Darlington*, *Selby* and *Harrogate* were surplus to requirements and moved to British Rail services, the latter two being sold to the London Midland Region (for Heysham-Belfast and Holyhead-Dublin) and the former initially going on charter to the Southern Region for their ailing Folkestone-Boulogne cargo service. However, it was not all retrenchment as efforts were made to expand the traffic by

The **Doric Ferry** was built at Ailsa Shipbuilding Co Ltd., Troon and entered service in 1962. *(Ferry Publications Library)*

modifying ships and installing new berths and allied infrastructure capable of dealing with unit-loads. The *Melrose Abbey* and *Bolton Abbey* were lengthened by 52ft and re-entered service from Hull to Rotterdam early in 1968 while the *Leeds* and the *Wakefield* were engaged on the Hull-Antwerp link.

Partners Argo Line introduced ro-ro vessels onto their Hull-Hamburg and Bremen routes in August 1967 thereby replacing AHL's *Darlington* while the Goole-Antwerp service succumbed in January 1968, the service from Hull effectively taking its place.

Control of the AHL passed from the Transport Holding Company to the National Freight Corporation in January 1969 but by now the writing was on the wall with AHL facing severe competition from both ro-ro and short-sea container operations. North Sea Ferries had introduced their nightly Hull-Rotterdam service in December 1965 and although critics had initially questioned its ability to survive, its success was both immediate and dramatic. By 1974, its twin vessels *Norwind* and *Norwave* were capacity constrained and larger ships were ordered. With just the Hull to Antwerp and Rotterdam services remaining, AHL's losses accrued and in November 1971, the service was finally wound up. It was left to the *Leeds* to close the Antwerp link while the *Melrose Abbey* closed the Rotterdam service on 29th November. AHL's failure to adapt to the changing traffic trends that were then sweeping through the short-sea ferry industry left them with no alternative but to withdraw.

Management of the three Eastern Region Humber paddle steamers was also transferred to AHL in 1959 and the ships adopted AHL's broad red band on their buff, black-topped funnels, but without the AHL letters. The three paddlers were repainted again in 1965, in the colours of British Rail but AHL remained as managers (see Chapter 8).

ATLANTIC STEAM NAVIGATION

Another notable associate company was the Atlantic Steam Navigation Company, a private concern nationalised in 1954.

The ASN was the brainchild of Frank Bustard, the White Star Line's Passenger Traffic Manager, who in 1934 had the intention to run an affordable Atlantic liner service following the merger of Cunard and the White Star. Financial constraints and the war hindered progress until 1946 when seeing the opportunity presented by war-surplus LSTs (Landing Ship, Tank), Lt Col Bustard took his Atlantic Steam Navigation Company in a quite different direction.

With a fleet of LSTs chartered from the Admiralty the company began operations between Tilbury and Hamburg in 1946. The service started with military charters returning material from Europe to England and the company progressed to providing commercial services across the Irish Sea and then across the North Sea.

In May 1948 the Atlantic Steam Navigation Company (ASN) acquired another LST which became the *Empire Doric* and was used to inaugurate a commercial service between Preston, Lancashire and Larne. This was the first commercial ro-ro ferry service in the world. It proved so successful that in 1950 the *Empire Gaelic* was acquired to operate a new service between Preston and Belfast.

After it was nationalised there was initially little or no change to ASN's operations, known as the Transport Ferry Service, although in 1955 another three LSTs were introduced, the *Empire Cymric*, *Empire Doric* and the *Empire Nordic*. In that

Top: Down the Swan, Hunter & Wigham Richardson ways at Walker goes the *Europic Ferry* on 10th October 1967. *(Ferry Publications Library)*

Above left: Afternoon drinks being served on the Sun Deck on the *Cerdic Ferry*. *(Ferry Publications Library)*

Above right: The First Class lounge on the *Cerdic Ferry*. *(Ferry Publications Library)*

Left: The vehicle deck of the *Cerdic Ferry* is a far cry from the vessels of the 21st Century. *(Ferry Publications Library)*

Has ever a ro-ro ferry looked so well? The magnificent ***Europic Ferry*** looking her best in the colours of the Atlantic Steam Navigation Company. *(Ferry Publications Library)*

year the service to Hamburg was also terminated and a new Tilbury-Antwerp route commenced. A significant development, however, came in 1956 when the entire fleet was taken over for Mediterranean use during the Suez crisis and the company's ro-ro operations were suspended until they returned in January 1957. In the interim, a token coaster service was provided at Preston. At this time the company was also given responsibility of a further 12 LSTs for use in Middle Eastern waters.

With such a large fleet of vessels engaged in the shipment of trucks the ASN very quickly identified ways of improving its operations. The chartered LSTs all loaded and unloaded vehicles through bow doors. How much better things would be if the door was in the stern of the vessel, where the hull was wider and if that door was also a ramp that could receive the shore bridge! The company was keen to explore the concept but finance was an issue. Under BTC control, however, ASN was able to realise its ro-ro ambitions with the introduction of the first UK-designed and purpose-built stern-loading vehicle ferry capable of accommodating trucks.

Built by the renowned Wm Denny and Brothers at Dumbarton, the *Bardic Ferry* could carry 70 trucks and 55 passengers in two classes. Interestingly the vehicle deck was strengthened to carry tanks, a requirement of the Ministry of Defence. Cargo was also accommodated on the upper deck and this was served by a 20-ton electric crane.

The new ferry entered service from Preston in September 1957 and was followed on the Larne run a year later by her sister *Ionic Ferry*, releasing the former for the Tilbury-Antwerp run.

A third ship, the slightly larger *Cerdic Ferry* arrived and entered service at Tilbury in 1961 allowing the *Bardic Ferry* to return to Preston. The 'Cerdic' was joined by her sister *Doric Ferry* in 1962, enabling a daily service and the withdrawal of the *Empire Cymric*.

It should be noted that the company had also built up a robust unit load business running between Preston and Larne as well as Ardrossan and Larne and run in close connection with the BTC's British Road Services Ltd. A twice-weekly service between Preston and Drogheda was launched in December 1961 and a daily service between Preston and Dublin followed

in March 1963. At one stage there were up to ten unit load ships employed on ASN Irish Sea routes.

Following the dissolution of the BTC in 1962, ownership of the ASN, like the AHL, was transferred to the Transport Holding Company and the fragile link between the company and the British Railways was severed. The Transport Act of 1968 saw another move, this time to the National Freight Corporation.

The handsome *Gaelic Ferry* was delivered in 1964 becoming the company's fifth purpose-built ship bringing capacity for over 100 trailers. Entering service at Tilbury, in July 1965 the ship moved to the new terminal developed by the company at the expanding port of Felixstowe.

By now the ASN's services were enjoying considerable success and to ensure continuity of operations during dry-docking periods the company turned to the charter market for relief tonnage. Discussions with Thoresen Ferries resulted in agreement to charter the smart and revolutionary *Viking II* in 1965, followed in 1966 and 1967 by the *Viking I*. The car ferries were employed on the Tilbury services but in January 1967 the *Viking I* actually appeared at Preston, running to Belfast rather than Larne.

Just under five years later the ASN was sold as part of the Conservative Government's policy of reprivatising viable nationalised companies. The ASN and its subsidiaries, the Transport Ferry Service (Nederland) NV and Frank Bustard and Sons Ltd, passed to the European Ferries Group. For £5.5million, the ASN's four routes, seven ferries and three terminals were merged with the Townsend Thoresen fleet.

The last ship ordered by the ASN was the *Europic Ferry*, the largest in the fleet. How well she looked in her smart livery of black-topped blue funnel with a broad white band, white upperworks and black hull nicely finished with a white stripe. On the bows was an arrow emblem, or fish tail, edged in blue which was also on the company's white house flag. It was an identity synonymous with high standards and style; an identity that would be lost in 1976 as the garish orange colours of Townsend Thoresen supplanted the colours once intended for an Atlantic Ocean dream.